WHAT PEOPLE ARE SAYING ABOUT

DEAD PE̶~

What a fine, thoughtful and qu   ...̶ ̶ about
Osama bin Laden], Saddam's enc   ̶ ̶ of death. It
moved and persuaded me, both.
Adam Gopnik, *New Yorker* Staff Writer, winner of three National
Magazine Awards and the George Polk Award for magazine
reporting

These tart, funny, sad, occasionally angry and always surprising
essays about recently departed writers, artists, musicians, and
terrorists are much more than obituaries. Taken together, they
form an intellectual, artistic, and political history of the 20th
century. It was, for the most part, a rotten century, but it's where
we came from, and very much worth revisiting through the eyes
and minds of Golberg and Meis.
Keith Gessen, co-editor of *n+1*, author of *All the Sad Young
Literary Men*

Read this book first for the tart, surprising sentences: "You could
call it a theological problem," on the Beastie Boys; "You can't
overestimate how difficult it is to write about McDonald's that
well," on Updike; "There is nowhere to stray when all is one," on
Tom Clancy, of all people. Then read it again to encounter two
minds beautifully surveying our hideous, glorious last century
passim. I both admire and teeth-grindingly envy this beautiful
little book.
Tom Bissell, *Harper's Magazine* Contributing Editor, Rome Prize,
Anna Akhmatova Prize

Are the essays collected here literary obituaries or just occasional
pieces (death being the final occasion for us all)? Whatever they

are they're smart, generous, honest, and probing. By giving equal attention and care to movie stars and terrorists and both famous and obscure intellectuals, Golberg and Meis offer us a bracing self-portrait of our time. In honoring the dead, they make us all feel more alive.

Gregory Wolfe, Editor, *Image Journal*

They say the dead are at the mercy of the living. Taking the measure of recently deceased notables, Golberg and Meis dazzle with their exuberant acumen, passionate range of interests, and, perhaps most remarkably, their empathy. Treasuring the arts and a life of the mind, they read the lives of the no-longer-with-us with phenomenally articulate, almost ecstatic joie de vivre.

Thomas Farber, author of *The End of My Wits*

The word 'eulogy' means, literally, 'to speak well,'" write Stefany Anne Golberg and Morgan Meis. They speak very well, but they do more than eulogize. Somehow, in distilled yet informal essays about these 29 people, they resurrect the deceased. This isn't eulogy. It's necromancy. In elegant prose, with the briefest of invocations, they summon before us Charlton Heston's charisma and Mikhail Kalashnikov's guilt. They contrast Chinua Achebe's anger toward and Joseph Conrad's pessimism about the West. The authors' unblinking eloquence triumphs especially in thoughtful looks at the deaths of Saddam Hussein and Osama bin Laden. "There is a kind of deep metaphysical democracy to Updike's prose," writes Meis in a tribute to the novelist, and the same embrace of diversity animates this volume. Name another party host who invited both Cy Twombly and Thomas Kinkade, or Tom Clancy and Kurt Cobain. It's a wonderful wake.

Michael Sims, author of *The Adventures of Henry Thoreau* and *The Story of Charlotte's Web*

Dead
People

Dead
People

Stefany Anne Golberg
and Morgan Meis

Winchester, UK
Washington, USA

First published by Zero Books, 2016
Zero Books is an imprint of John Hunt Publishing Ltd., Laurel House, Station Approach,
Alresford, Hants, SO24 9JH, UK
office1@jhpbooks.net
www.johnhuntpublishing.com
www.zero-books.net

For distributor details and how to order please visit the 'Ordering' section on our website.

Text copyright: Stefany Anne Golberg and Morgan Meis 2015

ISBN: 978 1 78535 336 9
Library of Congress Control Number: 2015956006

All rights reserved. Except for brief quotations in critical articles or reviews, no part of this
book may be reproduced in any manner without prior written permission from the publishers.

The rights of Stefany Anne Golberg and Morgan Meis as authors have been asserted in accordance
with the Copyright, Designs and Patents Act 1988.

A CIP catalogue record for this book is available from the British Library.

Design: Stuart Davies

Printed in the USA by Edwards Brothers Malloy

We operate a distinctive and ethical publishing philosophy in all
areas of our business, from our global network of authors to
production and worldwide distribution.

CONTENTS

Acknowledgements

Stefany Anne Golberg:

From *The Smart Set*: Václav Havel (previously published as "Always the Optimist"), 23 December 2011; Mikhail Kalashnikov (previously published as "Light and Shadow"), 11 February, 2014; Mary Ellen Mark (previously published as "Monsters and Men"), 13 July 2015; Thomas Kinkade (previously published as "Fade to Black"), 12 April, 2012; Roman Opalka (previously published as "Running the Numbers"), 19 August, 2011; David Weiss (previously published as "A Simple Story of Motion"), 8 June 2012; James van Sweden (previously published as "The Glory of the Garden"), 24 October 2013; Sun Ra (previously published as "A Cosmic Centennial"), 29 April 2014; Kurt Cobain (previously published as "The Sound of Despair"), 31 March 2014; Günter Grass (previously published as "Being Oskar Matzerath"), 8 June 2015.

Morgan Meis:

From *The Smart Set*: Eric Hobsbawm (previously published as "20th Century Man"), 9 October 2011; Leszek Kolakowski (previously published as "The Straight Talker"), 6 August 2009; Rsyzard Kapuscinski (previously published as "Was Ryszard Kapuscinski Beyond the Truth?"), 6 August 2007; Osama bin Laden (previously published as "The Smile"), 4 May 2011; Charlton Heston (previously published as "Charlton Heston's Last Act"), 8 April 2008; Robert Rauschenberg (previously published as "You Can't Take It With You"), 21 May 2008; Cy Twombly (previously published as "A Life of "E"s"), 8 July 2011; Robert Hughes (previously published as "Macho Man"), 17 August 2012; John Updike (previously published as "Updike the Synthesizer"), 2 February 2009; Chinua Achebe (previously published as "Heart of Lightness"), 15 April 2013; David Foster Wallace (previously published as "Dear David"), 19 September 2008; Tom Clancy (previously published as "Information Overload"), 15 October 2013; Adam Yauch (previously published as "Final Rap"), 14 May 2012; Guru (previously published as "Balancing Act"), 4 May 2010; Bob Bogle (previously published as "Surf's Up"), 23 June 2009.

From 3 *Quarks Daily*: Christopher Hitchens (previously published as "Remembering the Foolish and Brilliant Christopher Hitchens"), 19 December 2011; Susan Sontag (previously published as "Susan Sontag"), 26 June 2006.

From *n+1*: Arthur Danto (previously published as "The Miraculousness of the Commonplace"), 11 November 2013.

From *The New Yorker*: Tadeusz Konwicki (previously published as "To Be Alive and a Polish Writer: Tadeusz Konwicki, 1926–2015"), 12 February 2015.

Preface

We are drawn to famous people like moths to a flame. This is true across the board, from high culture to low, from arts to politics. We like to talk about the famous. We watch as their stories evolve. We compare ourselves to them. The life of a famous person has a way of shaping the meaning and worth of our own lives.

It is, therefore, momentous when a famous person dies. The death shocks us, interrupting the flow of everyday life. But more importantly, in death, the tables turn. It's our chance to judge the very people whose lives have been, implicitly, judging our own.

The word "eulogy" means, literally, "to speak well." Often, kind words about the dead are indeed uttered. But the kind words can be tinged with an element of revenge. More often than not, the work of eulogy is the work of reduction, of summing up. Aristotle once famously observed, citing the ancient Greek sage Solon, that a life can only be judged from the standpoint of its completion. Death, for Aristotle, is the bookend that allows us to see someone's life in its totality and to understand that life in a way impossible while the life is still in process. With the death of a famous person, the rest of us have the last word.

This Aristotelian approach to eulogy definitely provides its satisfactions. But in important aspects, it is wrong. That's because the attempts to judge a life end up saying more about the judge than the judged. The attempt to make pronouncements about another person's life, famous or otherwise, is never separate from the pronouncements we make upon our own lives. There is no neutral space. We're mired in bias before we even begin.

So, if the death of a human being is not the opportunity to judge that life or to sum it up, what makes a good eulogy? In the course of writing many eulogistic essays, we've come to the conclusion that the death of a fellow human being can be the opportunity to enter into that person's life. This sounds like a contradiction. How can death be the opportunity for life? But it is true, isn't it, that when someone dies it draws our collective attention to that person? We start to think about them more closely and more deeply than we did when they were alive. It's almost as if the person becomes more real by having so recently left us. That added dose of reality is a precious commodity. You could say that death gives us the chance truly to connect our own life with the life of the person who has died.

Perhaps this point can better be expressed with a metaphor of distance. The Aristotelian approach to eulogy requires an act of stepping back. To see the life of the dead person as a whole you must take a bird's eye view. From that distance, you hope to gain some clarity about the life in question. Our standpoint, by contrast, is to get in as close as we can. We've chosen to wear our bias on our sleeve. We've chosen to take these lives personally. In the face of the death of a person of influence, we've said, "We want to find out what made you tick now that you've stopped ticking."

Still, the inner core, the specific whatever-it-is that makes each human life so singularly and irreducibly that-which-it-is, will always remain a mystery. The essays in this volume circle respectfully around that mystery, tapping on a window here, peering through a doorway there. We hope to catch a glimpse, if only a glimpse, of what made these particular lives distinctive. These essays tend to be idiosyncratic, both in regards to the people we chose to write about and in the specific lens we affixed to our cameras to snap our little pictures. Some of the essays may be provocative. Others might catch you wrong-footed in terms of your expectations. We ask only that you come to them with an open mind. They do not pretend to be the last word on anyone or anything. They are simply our words, our words for a handful of dead people who, for whatever reason, meant something to us.

Christopher Hitchens

(1949 – 2011)

At the moment, I'm angry with Christopher Hitchens. Not because he died. A man dies. And angry is not really the correct word, nor the correct emotion. I'm frustrated with Christopher Hitchens, troubled by him, moved by him, enamored of him and then repelled at the attraction.

The first time I met Christopher Hitchens was at a *Harper's Magazine* Christmas party just before the start of the Iraq War. Bloomberg had recently banned smoking in New York City and the intellectuals were pissed. In those days, *Harper's* parties happened down in the basement at Pravda. It was all very arch. Smoking ban be damned. Lewis Lapham and his band of merry lit boys were going to light up the smokes anyway. Hitch had a Scotch in one hand and a cigarette in the other. But you've seen him like that a thousand times, in person, in pictures, on TV. I stood in line to speak with him. The line was moving smoothly until a woman in a red dress half a size too small for all her stuff gummed up the works. You could hear the collective groan all along the line as she stepped up to the Hitch. This was going to take a while.

I gave him a copy of a review a friend and I had written about his recently published book, *Letters to a Young Contrarian*. The book is not very good, a fact he readily acknowledged. Really, my friend and I wrote the review to attack him for his abandonment of the Left. He didn't care that we felt abandoned. Speaking with him, I came to understand that he really didn't care. All the same, he appreciated the review, which was pretty smart. Hitch appreciated smart. Always.

I suppose it was his confidence in leaving the Left behind that infected my own thinking after that meeting. He'd taken all his verve and passion and gone somewhere else. The real fight is with me, he kept saying, the good fight is with me. I'm a sucker for that kind of talk. I'm a sucker for a fist slammed on the table and a drunken rant about the genuine lost cause. It was around this time that a number of apostates on the Left were beginning to toy with the idea that being anti-fascist meant supporting any war that would rid the world of Saddam.

Anyway, I decided I was for the Iraq War too, and whatever else the new fight was going to entail, the grand struggle against all that is vile and inhuman. I signed up, if for no other reason than that I wanted to be with him.

Soon enough it became clear that the war had turned into a genuine debacle. When we all found out Hitch had cancer, I wondered if before died, he would say something about being wrong. A person can be wrong. Any person can be wrong. The facts don't turn out the way you hoped they would. Events turn ugly, turn sour, and history plays one of her infinite tricks, going one way just when you thought she was going the other. The Iraq War was a terrible mistake by any honest assessment and I, Morgan Meis, was wrong to have thought and argued differently. There. It isn't so hard to say. But Hitch could never say it. There was something greater at stake for him. There was something that he valued more deeply, in this case, than he valued the truth.

This is not at all to side with most of his critics, who happen to be smaller persons than he. There is no shame in being smaller than Christopher Hitchens. He was great. Most people are not great and are never going to be great no matter how hard they try. Arguing with greatness is an absurd undertaking. I can't tell you how many times I've watched Hitch demolish someone in discussion or debate when, in fact, the other party had the better argument, the more careful analysis. It doesn't matter with greatness. The force of greatness comes down like a cudgel. Everything is smashed when greatness comes barreling through.

It will be said a hundred times and then a hundred times more in the following weeks that Hitch's atheism was a stance of immense courage. This is complete bullshit. Hitch's atheism was a thing of anger and fear, and it fed off the anger and fear of the legions of angry and fearful religious people who took up the bait. Christopher Hitchens did not, for instance have the courage to confront the works of Simone Weil, and to read them with honesty and openness and a feeling for the greatness that is contained within her words. A person could read Simone Weil for a lifetime and never become a believer. But no honest person can read Simone Weil, truly read her, and maintain the position that religious belief is a phenomenon that can be dealt with solely in the mode of contempt. Christopher Hitchens was perfectly aware of this fact, which is why he never allowed himself genuinely to read the works of Simone Weil or genuinely to contemplate the paintings of Caravaggio or genuinely to recite the poems of Gerard Manley Hopkins, to pick a few random examples of greatness on this earth that, troublingly, cannot be disentangled from religion. There was something that Hitch valued more deeply, in this case too, than he valued the truth.

It will also be opined in the days and weeks to follow that Hitchens was a lover of reason and rationality. This is poppycock. Hitchens was a lover of argument and persuasion. He was a lover of being right and winning at any cost. This is what made him great. His irrationality made him shine. When the facts were out, and the facts were against him, it drove him to ever-more-eloquent flights of rhetoric in the name of his own doomed wrongness. This is not an admirable quality. In the hands of a lesser man, it would be pathetic. In the possession of a great man, however, such a quality cannot be judged so easily. It becomes a quality both wicked and grand. Hitch was large enough to take upon himself wickedness and grandness both. One of the reasons that we all loved to have Christopher Hitchens around is that he was proof that life does not always have to be so relentlessly disappointing, so boring. Being human does not always have to be a matter of being puny, of opting for the small matters of our own comfort day after day. Most of us live small lives of quiet desperation. Hitchens opted big every time. He paid the price for that choice, and never complained about it once.

When someone great leaves this earth you don't know what to do. I don't know what to do. It pains me that things will be said about Christopher Hitchens that have nothing to do with what actually made him great. Then again, this is as it should be. True human greatness is a thing that we do not get to measure. It is the thing that measures us. In his foolishness and brilliance Hitchens has established a measure that the rest of us now have to live with. We have to wrangle with it. We have to put our own lives as writers and thinkers and human beings against this massive thing that Christopher Hitchens has left behind. It is a hateful burden, this legacy. Still, it is as an honor that I bend down in order to lift up my own tiny portion. We all bear what part of it we can, the legacy of a great man. I'm angry with him. And I miss him very very much already.

By Morgan Meis
19 December 2011

Václav Havel

(1936 – 2011)

The recently deceased Václav Havel — writer, political dissident, and first president of the Czech Republic — wrote some very funny plays. Living through the dark times of communist Czechoslovakia, Havel was committed to keeping a sense of humor. Laughter, he felt, was not just an antidote to misery, an escape; it was a way to distance yourself from misery, gain a little perspective. This is the function of satire. Satire asks us to reflect on meaning, to ask what is truly meaningful and what is not. What do we take seriously because it is serious, and what do we take seriously because we've stopped asking questions?

These funny plays of Havel are generally classified as belonging to the absurdist tradition, alongside the works of Pinter, Albee, Stoppard, and Beckett. In the West, Havel's plays have represented all that is ridiculous and empty about communism in particular and bureaucracy and authority in general. Havel first came to international attention with *The Garden Party*. The play revolves around Mr. and Mrs. Pludek, who have middle-class aspirations for their two sons, Hugo and Peter. Dismissing Peter as a bourgeois intellectual, the Pludeks turn their attention to Hugo, who pleases his parents by becoming chief liquidator of the Liquidation Office. Hugo is told that the task of the Liquidation Office is to liquidate the Inauguration Office. Unfortunately, the Liquidation Office is also slated to be liquidated, and if it is liquidated it cannot liquidate. The capable Hugo finally becomes head of a new institution, the Central Committee for Inauguration and Liquidation, the purpose of which is liquidating liquidation. Because Hugo is smart and organized, he quickly adapts to his various bureaucratic roles, learning to speak the platitudinous, vacant language of his fellow functionaries. At the play's end, Hugo's identity is completely lost. Even his own parents no longer recognize him.

Havel's next play, *The Memorandum*, fully established him as a theatrical voice for Eastern Europeans living under the absurd logic of communism. *The Memorandum* begins in the office of Josef Gross. Gross is the managing director of the office, though what he manages, or what the office does, it is hard to say. It's a day like any other. Gross is reading his mail when he comes upon a memorandum in a language he does not understand. He is then informed by his secretary that the memo is written in a Ptydepe, a new language that has been introduced by the deputy director Jan Ballas, without Gross' knowledge or consent. Ptydepe, it is explained to Gross, is a more efficient and reliable language for the office because it is more redundant, ridding language of unwieldy similarities and also emotional connotations. All words, for instance, must differ from words of similar length by 60 percent. Gross at first protests against the introduction of Ptydepe, but is later convinced by Gross that Ptydepe is best for everyone. Nonetheless, Gross still does not understand Ptydepe, and spends the play in an exasperating attempt to get the memo translated. First he needs permission. He is told to get authorization from the graduate Ptydepist, and then, actually, from the Chairman, who, it turns out, does not herself have authorization. He asks a secretary named Maria to help him, but she tells Gross that while she can translate the memo, she does not have the proper permit to do so. And the whole time, of course, Gross is being watched by George, the staff watcher. In the end, Ptydepe is replaced with another new language, Chorukor, and then it is agreed that everyone will, in fact, go back to the mother language. Then everyone goes to lunch.

In his 1990 book *Disturbing the Peace: A Conversation with Karel Huizdala,* Havel wrote: "The deeper the experience of an absence of meaning — in other words, of absurdity — the more energetically meaning is sought." Born into a wealthy, intellectual Prague family in 1936, the rise of communism in then-Czechoslovakia cancelled many of the privileges that would have been afforded to the young Havel. Because of his "bourgeois" background, Havel was prevented from attending university. He worked for a time as a lab technician, and then studied at a technical college before serving in the Czechoslovak Army in the late 1950s. But all the while, Havel maintained an interest in literature. He began to write in earnest and involved himself in various literary circles. In the 1960s, he got work in a theater as a stagehand and started to write his own plays. After the Prague Spring reforms were crushed in 1968, Havel became increasingly immersed in the political struggle against communism. His arrest in 1979, and his life as a public dissident in Czechoslovakia, ran parallel to his life as an internationally known playwright. Soon, Havel became the world's most visible Czech dissident. And after the fall of the Berlin Wall in 1989, this privileged-yet-disenfranchised famous artist and political revolutionary became president of Czechoslovakia. He resigned in 1992 only to be elected president again the following year — of the newly created Czech Republic.

In the decades that followed, Václav Havel, the playwright turned politician, became one of those go-to public figures when someone needed a voice of authority on aesthetic freedom or political revolution. Yet Havel's guidance rarely focused on either politics or aesthetics. The problem of creating real and lasting societal change, was, for Havel, a moral dilemma. And absurdity was the path through this moral problem. Havel did not see absurdity as something that people in power impose on the powerless. He did not see the absurd as that which is devoid of purpose, as Eugéne Ionesco said. Havel saw absurdity as a fact of life, and the embrace of absurdity — the experience of meaninglessness — as the necessary condition by which we find meaning. Modern man, he wrote in *Disturbing the Peace*, needed to descend the spiral of his own absurdity to the lowest point. Only then could he look beyond it, only then could he discover real meaning. Havel's plays are not critiques of "systems," of authority figures and illogical bosses and the tedium of office life. Havel's plays are a critique of us, of all of us, those in charge and those under charge, who created all the absurd and meaningless structures of modern society we lament on a daily basis, feel so oppressed by, and yet refuse to change.

"Lie" is a word Havel used often in one of his most discussed and influential essays, 1978's "The Power of the Powerless." He wrote:

> In everyone there is some longing for humanity's rightful dignity, for moral integrity, for free expression of being and a sense of transcendence over the world of existence. Yet, at the same time, each person is capable, to a greater or lesser degree, of coming to terms with living within the lie. Each person somehow succumbs to a profane trivialization of his inherent humanity, and to utilitarianism. In everyone there is some willingness to merge with the anonymous crowd and to flow comfortably along with it down the river of pseudolife.

For those who haven't read the essay, or haven't read it in a long time, the word "powerless" in the title might suggest those suffering under communism, the masses, or perhaps all people who are in a power struggle against authority. But the essay is much more existential and much less political than that. For Havel, the modern world was in spiritual crisis. "As soon as man began considering himself the source of the highest meaning in the world and the measure of everything, the world began to lose its human dimension, and man began to lose control of it," he wrote in *Disturbing the Peace*. The modern project to make humans more powerful — more in control of our environment, of nature, each other — resulted, rather, in a loss of power, a loss of meaning. And the deeper we experience the absence of meaning, "the more energetically meaning is sought."

This is the point when individual people, alienated and lacking purpose, become susceptible to ideology, to placing their trust in an anonymous Power that offers them comfort, even if that comfort is a lie. It's not even necessary that people believe in the lies they are told; they only need to behave as if they do, to conform to its logic. In return, the lie offers not just a new politics; it offers a new mythology, a new identity, a new language, a new metaphysics.

That willingness to float down the river of pseudolife is a problem common to all individuals, and is not reserved for the powerful or the weak or the doltish. "Individuals confirm the system, fulfill the system, make the system, are the system." To prove his point, Havel made the main character in "The Power of the Powerless" a greengrocer — an innocent shopkeeper, who only wants to sell us fruit and vegetables. The greengrocer is a prototype of the average person who longs for meaning and allows his moral vacuum to be filled with easy, empty ideology.

The manager of a fruit-and-vegetable shop places in his window, among the onions and carrots, the slogan: "Workers of the world, unite!" Why does he do it? What is he trying to communicate to the world? Is he genuinely enthusiastic about the idea of unity among the workers of the world? Is his enthusiasm so great that he feels an irrepressible impulse to acquaint the public with his ideals? Has he really given more than a moment's thought to how such a unification might occur and what it would mean?

Note the way Havel chose to specifically critique "unification." In the ideological fight against communism waged by the dissidents of the Eastern Bloc, the idea of unity — solidarity — was the weapon of choice. True solidarity, thought Havel, versus the false solidarity of the communist regime, was the basis from which change would spring. And yet, Havel wrote the word "unity" almost as if it were a dirty word. The reason is this: Unity was also a slogan of communist ideology. Indeed, all authorities declare a comforting message of unity. This is the primary function of ideology, he wrote. To provide people, "both as victims and pillars of the post-totalitarian system, with the illusion that the system is in harmony with the human order and the order of the universe."

Havel felt that the whole world, East and West, was caught in a conflict "between an impersonal, anonymous, irresponsible, and uncontrollable juggernaut of power" posing as a harmonic universe, and "the elemental and original interests of man as a concrete individual." When human beings experienced a loss of "superpersonal moral authority," they no longer saw themselves as part of a true unity — a universal unity. Conformity took the place of responsibility. Science in the 20th century had shown us something in the universe greater than ourselves, but it offered no direction. "Today," he said in a 1994 speech in Philadelphia titled "The Need for Transcendence in the Postmodern World," "we may know immeasurably more about the universe than our ancestors did, and yet, it increasingly seems they knew something more essential about it than we do, something that escapes us. The same thing is true of nature and of ourselves."

A deeper sense of individual responsibility toward the world would only be awakened in people when they directed themselves toward some kind of higher moral authority. In other words, unity and freedom will be achieved when people undergo a metaphysical transformation. This is what differentiates real unity from totalitarianism.

Václav Havel's emphasis on the "moral reconstitution of society" is perhaps the most revolutionary, and most overlooked, aspect of his legacy. As an icon for Western leftist intellectuals, the religious implications of a moral revolution caused some understandable discomfort and confusion. But Havel mistrusted a social unity based solely on politics, and rejected the idea that politics would remedy the crises of modern civilization.

Havel once said that the true dissident is not interested in power, has no desire for office and does not gather votes. It's an ironic statement coming from a future president. The absurdity of his own rise to power has been pointed out numerous times, first and foremost by Havel himself. Whether or not he lived up to his own values as a politician, Havel always felt that the role of a leader should be no different than the role of a dissident — a leader should simply be a voice for the people. The only kind of politics that makes sense, said Havel, is one that is guided by conscience. Political institutions should be open, dynamic and small, rather than closed, inviolable and huge. "It is better to have organizations springing up ad hoc," he wrote in "The Power of the Powerless," "infused with enthusiasm for a particular purpose and disappearing when that purpose has been achieved." In other words, institutions are best when they serve a specific purpose, and are not a replacement for community. And they are best when they place moral concerns before political ones. Without addressing the spiritual needs of people, without focusing on real human relationships and personal trust, democracy was likely to be just as absurd as communism. In this, Havel was much more radical than most of his post-democracy peers, at least intellectually. He was a politician who saw good politics as a result rather than a solution.

In his heart, Havel was always an optimist. The profound downward spiral into absurdity at the core of the greengrocer's — and society's — crisis was also their greatest hope. "Isn't it the moment of most profound doubt that gives birth to new certainties? Perhaps hopelessness is the very soil that nourishes human hope; perhaps one could never find sense in life without first experiencing its absurdity." You could say Havel's philosophy of change was based less on the "power of the people," and more so on the power of the person.

On the day of Havel's death, Czech novelist Milan Kundera said, "Václav Havel's most important work is his own life."

There's a moral there somewhere, one that Havel would have appreciated very much indeed.

By Stefany Anne Golberg
23 December 2011

Eric Hobsbawm

(1917 – 2012)

I studied briefly with Eric Hobsbawm, the English Marxist historian who died October 1st at the age of 94. I studied with him in the early 1990s at The New School for Social Research in New York City. Hobsbawm was just completing his book *The Age of Extremes*, the third in a trilogy that included *The Age of Capital* and *The Age of Empire*. Hobsbawm was not an inspiring teacher. He would shuffle into the classroom in his baggy suit and sit down at a table at the head of the class. Then he would open up a folder and begin to read us chapters from the book he was trying to finish. That was it. Hobsbawm didn't read very well. A strange-looking man, his mouth was always screwed up to the right. He mumbled out of the side of his face. The great German philosopher Jürgen Habermas would sometimes show up for a lecture or a conference at The New School during those days as well. Due to Habermas' severe lisp, you could barely understand him either. I suspect a generation of grad students formed the opinion that academic greatness and the inability to speak were somehow related. I recently read a passage from one of Hobsbawm's books where he reflects on his love of jazz. The book is called *Interesting Times: A Twentieth Century Life*. In it, Hobsbawm wrote:

Like the Czech writer Josef Skvorecky, who has written better about it than most, I experienced this musical revelation at the age of first love, 16 or 17. But in my case it virtually replaced first love, for, ashamed of my looks and therefore convinced of being physically unattractive, I deliberately repressed my physical sensuality and sexual impulses. Jazz brought the dimension of wordless, unquestioning physical emotion into a life otherwise almost monopolised by words and the exercises of the intellect.

Thinking back to the man in his early 70s reading to his students from his then soon-to-be-published book, it occurs to me that Hobsbawm was still that 16- or 17-year-old kid. I ran into him once at the A&P supermarket on Union Square. He had a few items in his shopping cart and was wandering around in the aisles. When I spoke to him he looked at me shyly from under his brow. I asked him a few questions about the Third International. He looked relieved. Yes, let us speak of the Third International. Why is it that I will forever associate Eric Hobsbawm with the feeling of embarrassment? It can't be his fault alone. It must have to do with me, too. It must touch on my own youthful Marxism and the naïve idealism it entailed, memories of conversations in smoky apartments during another time. Memories that now make me wince. What did any of us actually mean by "permanent revolution?"

Hobsbawm never recanted his communism though, not like I did, not like the rest of us. I remember wishing that he would. It was embarrassing for the rest of us that he kept up his support for the Soviet Union even after its demise. But I've come to understand that it was different for him. He was born in 1917, after all. He was a 20th-century man. Mass political movements are one thing that defines the 20th century. The working class arrived as a political entity in the beginning of the 20th century and died as one by the end. The Soviet Union represented the idea — though as Hobsbawm himself admitted, never the reality — that the working class could take political power and fashion a new society. He once said, in his typically laconic manner, "I belong to the generation for whom the October Revolution represented the hope of the world." Generations, millions of people, lived out their lives under the umbrella of that dream. Over time, Eric Hobsbawm became a human symbol of that dream. And he was aware that this made him fully an anachronism by 1989. Hobsbawm claimed that he was never much of an idealist. His support of the Soviet Union was not fired by romantic enthusiasm. And so, he could witness the passing away of the communist regime he never really liked on a personal level with the same reserve with which he supported it. In an interview with Tristam Hunt of *The Observer* in 2002, Hobsbawm explained it like this:

> Why I stayed in the Communist Party is not a political question about communism, it's a one-off biographical question. It wasn't out of idealisation of the October Revolution. I'm not an idealiser. One should not delude oneself about the people or things one cares most about in one's life. Communism is one of these things and I've done my best not to delude myself about it even though I was loyal to it and to its memory. The phenomenon of communism and the passion it aroused is specific to the twentieth century.

That is an interesting thing for a historian to say, that the passion aroused by communism was specific to the 20th century. As a historian, Hobsbawm was forced, in his analysis, to take an objective stance, to look at history from a position above the fray. But he also seems to have realized that real history only happens when people are within the fray. History had made him a communist and he was going to stay that way. Hobsbawm didn't try to be wiser than his own times. He didn't believe he could out-think the 20th century. He was content to be a living document of one of the defining forces of his era. Self-aware all the way to the end, he was never embarrassed. He never shirked from the implications. He never wanted anyone else to be embarrassed for him.

In a *New York Times* review of Hobsbawm's *Interesting Times: A Twentieth Century Life*, Christopher Hitchens admitted a grudging admiration for Hobsbawm. Given Hitchens' usual disgust for figures of the communist Left, who he generally dismissed as apologists for Totalitarianism, it was a surprising position. "Hobsbawm's vices," Hitchens wrote, "mutate into his virtues." Hitchens too was struck by the trudging stubbornness of Old Man Hobsbawm. Maybe Hitchens saw in Hobsbawm a perfect foil to himself. It was always Hitchens' fantasy that he could stay one step ahead of the march of history. Here in Hobsbawm was a man who practically reveled in the fact that he had been left behind. Ahead or behind, history has managed to make both of them look foolish. Hobsbawm had decided it was best to be exactly what he was. He was a shy and strange-looking kid who loved jazz and communism. A 20th-century man.

By Morgan Meis
9 October 2011

Leszek Kolakowski

(1927 – 2009)

Leszek Kolakowski died a couple of weeks ago. He was a philosopher, a man of letters, a historian of ideas. He lived the 20th-century life. It sucked. But like many a Pole, he made the best of a bad situation. The opening lines of the Polish National Anthem are, after all, "Poland has not perished yet." Poles know that everything will turn out for the worst. It always does.

Kolakowski grew up during the Nazi occupation of Poland and came of age when the Nazis were exchanged for the Soviets. Liberation, in Poland, is the name for a short period of chaos between oppressors. Kolakowski did his best to think with the times. He started out a Marxist — not a ridiculous position for a young anti-fascist to take in those days. It was not, however, a position that any self-respecting Eastern European could hold past the mid-'50s. Kolakowski had some self-respect.

That's where it gets interesting. Never an either/or sort of fellow, Kolakowski opted for nuance. There were things about the Socialist mindset that he liked. He also considered himself fundamentally Conservative. It's a tricky position, a perfect place from which to be misunderstood by everyone, on every side. For better or worse, Kolakowski was too smart to care. He wrote a unique essay that tried to make sense of this precarious intellectual standpoint. It is short, bold, and brilliant. He called it "Conservative/Liberal/Socialist."

It's impossible to be a Conservative/Liberal/Socialist. Except that Kolakowski did it. His argument is so simple and so obvious that it has never really caught on. Smart people like complicated shit and fancy words. Only truly brilliant people like Kolakowski are able to stop being so damn fancy and get back to simplicity.

Kolakowski's essay is a model of concision. Its three central propositions can be summed up with the following:

First, Kolakowski is a Conservative because there is "no happy ending in human history" and "we would do well to expect the worst." This also comes from the Pole in him. That good ol' Enlightenment idea that we will improve man through better institutions strikes him as dubious at best. Usually, we screw things up. So, better to back off than to give ammunition to those who would make of society a giant corrective Gulag. And there is always some brilliant monster out there perfectly happy to do just that.

Second, Kolakowski is a Liberal because he believes that the State has a role. If nothing else, it guarantees a base level of security. This security creates an arena in which people can compete for goods and services and generally go about the business of being human. It ain't grand, but it works, more or less. Much human misery will still exist but, after all, "to make people happy is not the function of the State."

Third, Kolakowski is a Socialist because he doesn't see massive social inequality as a good thing simply because it exists. Don't be so conservative that you end up justifying every shitty way that people get over on one another as the natural order of things. Or as Kolakowski nicely puts it, "The kind of conservative anthropological pessimism which led to the astonishing belief that a progressive income tax was an inhuman abomination is just as suspect as the kind of historical optimism on which the Gulag Archipelago was based." Social mechanisms that create a more level playing field can be very nice indeed. It is not impossible for us to be nice to each other sometimes.

Having made these three points, Kolakowski finishes with this:

So far as I can see, this set of regulative ideas is not self-contradictory. And therefore it is possible to be a conservative-liberal-socialist. This is equivalent to saying that those three particular designations are no longer mutually exclusive options.

Clean, laconic, sane. Every time I read the essay I'm reminded of the fact that it is damn wise. A wise man passed from this Earth a few weeks ago. Of course, he'd have been the first to agree that no one will really care.

By Morgan Meis
6 August 2009

Tadeusz Konwicki

(1926 – 2015)

I will never forget a late-night conversation I had seven years ago, around the table of a modest kitchen in a small town in southern Poland, when an impressively inebriated man — a distant relative — implored me with tear-filled eyes to get the message to Obama, as quickly as possible, that a missile shield pointed east, at Moscow, was a dire necessity. Every morning, this man told me, he looked to the east and expected to see Russian hordes cresting the hill just beyond the outskirts of his defenseless town. Then he pointed his finger at the window. We both looked out warily into the night.

There is a special mix of vindictiveness, paranoia, and persecution complex that can bubble to the surface in countries that have been betrayed too often. The opening line to the Polish National Anthem — "Poland has not yet perished" — gives you a good impression of the national disposition. Many Poles, even 20 years after the fall of Communism, live in a state of fatalistic, half-amused anticipation, waiting for the other shoe to drop. Historically, it's been the Russians who come to administer the boot. This happened, for instance and notoriously, in the January uprising of 1863, when Poles started a rebellion against forced conscription into the Imperial Russian Army. The rebellion ended, as many did, in misery and mass executions. And don't even get a Pole started about the partitions of the late 18th century, in which Russia, Prussia, and Austria carved Poland up into so many pieces that there was no independent state left.

Tadeusz Konwicki, who died last month, wrote fiction that is steeped in this history, in these agonies and conundrums. His great novel *The Polish Complex* begins like this: "I was standing in line in front of a state-owned liquor store. I was twenty-third in line." The book was written in the late 1970s, in a Poland behind the Iron Curtain and two decades removed from the brave, foolish, and short-lived Poznan Uprising against Soviet domination, in 1956. The entire novel takes place in line on Christmas Eve. Standing in that line, waiting to buy goods that never arrive, is Konwicki himself. Just behind him is a Polish man who has been waiting for an opportunity to kill Konwicki since the Second World War. "I owe you a bullet," the man says to Konwicki. "A slug in the back of the head." "I know," responds Konwicki. "I betrayed the old faith for the new one. Then the new one for the old. But I never wanted to betray anything or anybody."

The end of the Second World War replayed the ongoing tragedy of Polish independence — or, rather, the lack thereof: having painfully thrown off the yoke of Nazi occupation, Poles watched as the Soviets marched in to fill the power vacuum and set up shop. Konwicki himself was a party to these events. As a young man, he'd joined the Home Army and was involved in the double-jeopardy game of armed resistance both to the Wehrmacht and the R.K.K.A. (Red Army). Konwicki was a soldier fighting in the forests around his home town of Wilno (now Vilnius, the capital of Lithuania). Somehow, he survived. He moved to Warsaw and began a career as a writer within the indirectly Moscow-directed new Poland of the Cold War era.

And that is why the man in line outside the state-owned liquor store in *The Polish Complex* wants to kill Konwicki: he sees him as a traitor to the true cause of absolute freedom for Poland. He sees Konwicki's writing as veiled excuses for Konwicki's "collaboration" in a compromised Poland that was unable to throw off Russian domination in the aftermath of the Second World War. The man in line is, you guessed it, Konwicki's own conscience, which vexes him day and night.

Konwicki and his conscience step away from the line to drink vodka and talk about the bad old times. On several occasions,

Konwicki falls into a swoon, from drink and a bad heart, and dreams about failed uprisings from Poland's past, or about amorous adventures with the bored young woman sitting behind the desk at the store. Always, he awakens surrounded by his countrymen, freezing cold, waiting in line to buy something for Christmas. Finally, at the end of the novel... well, I won't spoil it.

Perhaps the most moving aspect of *The Polish Complex* is the degree to which Konwicki struggles not to have to struggle with the heavy burden of Polish history. Konwicki didn't want to be faced with the daily moral dilemmas that confront a person who lives in a country ruled by a rotten regime. Who does? He realizes that an obsession with historical resentments is poisonous and corrosive to the soul. "How did it happen?" Konwicki asks himself,

> that I am the author of Polish books, good or bad, but Polish? Why did I accept the role which I had renounced forever? Who turned me, a European, no, a citizen of the world, an Esperantist, a cosmopolitan, an agent of universalism, who turned me, as in some wicked fairytale, into a stubborn, ignorant, furious Pole?

Konwicki has no answer to these questions. The novel simply breaks here and begins a new section in which Konwicki and his friends are back in line, waiting endlessly for a shipment of goods and knowing that word of the shipment is probably just a rumor.

Soon enough, *The Polish Complex* returns to its central questions: What is it to be alive? Worse, what is it to be alive and Polish? Worse yet, what is it to be alive and a Polish writer? The book's creeping realization is that history can't be wished away. The memories, the moral dilemmas, do not disappear. The wounds of the 20th century were too many and too powerful, and Konwicki was never able to turn his back on those traumas. Instead, he returned to the scarring events of his past again and again in his writings (and in the movies he wrote and directed, including *The Last Day of Summer* and *Salto*). This was his modest act of literary heroism.

Konwicki never spared himself. He says in *The Polish Complex* that he was "molded from three different clays. And then fired in the temperature inferno of three elements. The clays were Polish, Lithuanian, and Belorussian, and the elements were Polish, Russianness, and Judaism, or, more precisely, Jewishness." He used his own battered psyche as a testing ground for the potential survival of the Polish soul.

Somewhere in the middle of *The Polish Complex*, Konwicki's conscience directs at him the following lines:

I am your judge. I've read everything you ever dished up. I have a bookshelf where I keep you under lock and key, because your work is such a fleeting thing. It hangs on the thread of the moment. You are a temporary writer. Your books will die with you.

This, no doubt, is what Konwicki often felt about himself as a writer. But in writing those thoughts down so honestly he overcame them. Tadeusz Konwicki, a Polish writer, died last month. But his books did not die with him.

By Morgan Meis
12 February 2015

Mikhail Kalashnikov

(1919 – 2013)

Among the displays of assault rifles at the Mikhail Kalashnikov Museum in Izhevsk is a small lawnmower Kalashnikov designed to push about the grounds of his summer cottage. It is said that Mikhail Kalashnikov loved to care for his grass. Kalashnikov gave the lawnmower the same sensible qualities he gave the gun that bears his name. The lawnmower is light, simple, cheap to construct and easy to hold—something a child could use.

Kalashnikov didn't regret inventing the Kalashnikov rifle. "I invented it for the protection of the Motherland," he said. Still, he once mused that he would like to have been known as a man who helped farmers and gardeners. "I wanted to invent an engine that could run forever," Kalashnikov once said. "I could have developed a new train, had I stayed in the railway." But this was not to be.

Mikhail Kalashnikov was born in the rural locality of Kurya, the 17th child of peasants. When Kalashnikov was still a boy, his family's property was confiscated and they were deported to Western Siberia. The farming was hard there, but harder was the shame of being exiled from the Soviet workers' paradise. Kalashnikov was a sickly child and though his studies didn't take him past secondary school, the future inventor dreamed of being a poet. After finishing the seventh grade, young Kalashnikov gathered his poetry books and worked as a technician on the Turkestan-Siberian railway, until he was conscripted into the Red Army in 1938. He worked with tanks and, in his spare time, tinkered with small arms. In 1941, Kalashnikov was wounded in battle. There, in the hospital, suffering from war wounds and shellshock, Kalashnikov had his vision. "I decided to build a gun of my own which could stand up to the Germans," he would later say. "It was a bit of a crazy escapade, I suppose. I didn't have any specialist education and I couldn't even draw." At first, Kalashnikov had trouble finding attention for his designs, but as his story continues, we find him persevering. By 1949, Kalashnikov's 7.62mm assault rifle was adopted by the Soviet Army. The shy Mikhail Kalashnikov, 30 years old, was awarded the Stalin Prize for Industrial Work. Later, the son of peasant farmers would become known as a Hero of Socialist Labor.

Had Mikhail Kalashnikov died in the war, he would never have known the results of his invention. But, as it turned out, Mikhail Kalashnikov lived a very long time. He lived to see millions killed with AK-47s. Perhaps just as devastating, he saw millions become killers. The killers were often people with whom Kalashnikov otherwise stood — the poor, the vulnerable, those deserving to be liberated from oppression. But the AK-47 was popular with everybody — warlords, assassins, criminals. Even so, Kalashnikov felt the positive effects of the gun outweighed the negative. "I sleep soundly," he told *The Guardian* in 2003. "The fact that people die because of an AK-47 is not because of the designer, but because of politics." Yet Kalashnikov was not without reflection. "I'm proud of my invention," he relented, "but I'm sad that it is used by terrorists." "When I see how peaceful people are killed and wounded by these weapons," he told *The Times* in 2006, "I get very distressed and upset. I calm down by telling myself that I invented this gun 60 years ago to protect the interests of my country."

Over the long years, people would forget about the inventor Mikhail Kalashnikov. And then an AK-47 would end up in a news story, next to a teenager in the Ivory Coast maybe, and people would ask him again, "Are you troubled by your invention?"

Upon the death of Mikhail Timofeyevich Kalashnikov at the age of 94, was the revelation of a letter, written by Kalashnikov to the head of Russia's Orthodox Church with the help of his local priest. The letter, typed onto Kalashnikov's home stationary, was published by the Russian paper *Izvestia* and patchy translations soon found their way into the international media. It was the anguished confession of a terrified old man on his deathbed.

"My spiritual pain is unbearable," he wrote,

> I keep asking the same insoluble question. If my rifle deprived people of life then can it be that I … a Christian and an orthodox believer, was to blame for their deaths?
>
> Yes! An increasing number of churches and monasteries in our land. And yet evil does not decrease! … Light and shadow, good and evil, two opposites of a whole, that can't exist without each other?

At the bottom of the letter he finished, "Slave of God, designer Mikhail Kalashnikov," and scrawled his signature to seal it.

* * *

There are two prevailing ideas about invention. The first is that it comes from necessity, as in the well-known saying, "Necessity is the mother of invention." Technology, in this case, is a direct extension of human need. The Soviets liked this definition, liked to think of machines as the reward of an enlightened people, birthed directly from pure, unadulterated purpose, a purpose that led directly to progress. As one Stalinist propaganda campaign explained: "The Party and Workers Should Master Technology …Technology Decides All."

The second definition of invention is that it is the product of pure imagination. In this understanding, invention is strictly for its own sake, and is its own justification. Invention is an act of creating. Too much focus on results is detrimental to creation. Here, the inventor is a small god, magically pulling contraptions out of the void.

The author Mary Shelley had a third understanding of invention. "Invention, it must be humbly admitted," she wrote in the 1831 Preface to *Frankenstein*, does not consist in creating out of void but out of chaos … the materials must, in the first place, be afforded: it can give form to dark, shapeless substances, but cannot bring into being the substance itself." In the Shelleyan explanation, invention doesn't come from nothingness or need. The inventor is neither a hero whose inventions are venerated nor a god whose inventions are beside the point. The Shelleyan inventor is a translator, an interpreter between nature and human desire.

Whether it's a lawnmower or a locomotive or an AK-47, the inventor is always faced with the same burden — how to turn chaos into order. But the chaos the inventor faces is not only the chaos of nature; it is also the chaos of human desire. The inventor stands between these two forces, pulled in both directions, servant to both nature and man.

So, as every invention is a translation of nature, it is also a battle with it. Maybe it's better to say that every invention is a re-ordering of nature according to people's tastes at any given time. How can we best shape the grass? How can we move through space and time faster? How can we kill more efficiently?

There must be, I think, something illuminated about the lifeworld of the inventor. I imagine the inventor sees an animated world, where all the things of being — organic and inorganic — are part of the same universal soul. For people who use objects and don't make them, meaning and value come after the thing. But for an inventor, the meaning comes before the material. "I wanted to invent an engine that could run for ever," Kalashnikov said. "I could have developed a new train, had I stayed in the railway." And then he said of his train, "It would have looked like the AK-47 though." For an inventor like Mikhail Kalashnikov, a train is just as much an extension of our humanity as a lawnmower or a gun. They are just different shapes of chaos.

Deep within the soul of the inventor is a yearning — to be a bridge between the visible and the invisible, the natural and the mechanical. This is a large burden, because so much gets lost in translation. The dangerous consequences of invention are not separate from its amazing results; sometimes they are indistinguishable. Kalashnikov said it himself: Light and shadow, good and evil, two opposites of a whole, that can't exist without each other. It's not so far from what Victor Frankenstein said of his magnificent wretched Creature: "I had desired it with an ardour that far exceeded moderation; but now that I had finished, the beauty of the dream vanished, and breathless horror and disgust filled my heart." If there's one thing Mary Shelley wanted to tell us in her book it is this: Victor Frankenstein never sets out to make a monster. He sees himself as a beacon in the darkness, an explorer seeking to reveal "the outward substance of things or the inner spirit of nature and the mysterious soul of man." Victor Frankenstein doesn't fashion his Creature ex nihilo; the Creature is an extension of his own humanity, the materialization of his ambition. Indeed, Victor Frankenstein sees the Creature as a fulfillment of the aspirations of all humankind.

In the letter he wrote to the Orthodox Church — so much like the confession of Victor Frankenstein to Robert Walton — Mikhail Kalashnikov speaks of his AK-47, his Creature, as a "miracle weapon." There is danger at the core of every invention, no matter what it is. We think we are creating miracles with our inventions but, at the same time, we are creating monsters, too. In other words, the story of the AK-47 is not simply whether guns are inherently good or bad. Nor is it whether they can become good in the right hands and evil in the wrong hands. It is, rather, that an invention will always, eventually, rage out of its inventor's control. The inventor never controlled it in the first place.

"It was like a genie out of the bottle," Kalashnikov said of his weapon, "and it began to walk all on its own and in directions I did not want."

* * *

All this translation takes a toll on the soul of the inventor. The obsession with vulcanizing rubber brought Charles Goodyear and his family to ruin. Wallace Carothers, the chemist who invented Nylon, once listed for a colleague at DuPont all the famous chemists who had committed suicide. And then, after taking a fatal dose of cyanide in 1937, he added his own name to the list. The dapper pioneer of flight Alberto Santos-Dumont, who liked to fly his marvelous dirigibles around Paris, ended his days hanging from a pipe in a hotel room in Guarujá. Jack Parsons developed the rocket fuel that launched the United States into space and called himself the Antichrist. "The mainspring of an individual is his creative Will," he wrote.

> This Will is the sum of his tendencies, his destiny, his inner truth. It is one with the force that makes the birds sing and flowers bloom; as inevitable as gravity, as implicit as a bowel movement, it informs alike atoms and men and suns.
>
> To the man who knows this Will, there is no why or why not, no can or cannot; he IS!
>
> There is no known force that can turn an apple into an alley cat; there is no known force that can turn a man from his Will. This is the triumph of genius; that, surviving the centuries, enlightens the world.

"This force burns in every man," wrote Jack Parsons, and then blew himself up in his home.

"Man keeps inventing things all the time," said the designer Mikhail Kalashnikov. "Life is composed of different inventions." How true his statement is. As much as inventions come out of the inventor's hands, they are, in the end, form to the dark shapelessness of all life. Remember, Shelley warned us in her story, inventors only give form to substance. They cannot bring into being the substance itself. The form of Mikhail Kalashnikov's invention was an AK-47. But the substance of his invention is us.

By Stefany Anne Golberg
11 February 2014

Rsyzard Kapuscinski

(1932 – 2007)

It's a shame the 20th century was such an unrelenting nightmare. Especially if you were anywhere near Central or Eastern Europe (though by no means exclusively so). Those who perished more often than not perished in suffering and fear. Those who lived had to make do.

"Making do" could mean a lot of things. Keeping your mouth shut while the Nazis rounded up everyone else on the block. Mentioning something you overheard your neighbor say to the local Stasi agent to deflect suspicion from yourself. Perhaps outright collaboration with the secret police. It was a dirty business, and it reached down deep. We like to pretend of ourselves and our heroes that there was a way to remain untainted. But that was the cruel genius of the police states of the 20th century. Whether out of Soviet or National Socialist motivations the point of the total state was to reach into every crevice, every nook and cranny of the lifeworld, every aspect of a personality and a social structure. The aim was to control everything and to make everyone complicit. Everything. Everyone.

The recent revelations about Nobel Laureate Günter Grass having served with an SS Unit at the end of World War II and famed writer Ryszard Kapuscinski having sometimes played informant for the SB (the Polish Secret Police) further confirm the point. But this doesn't lessen the blow. These are depressing revelations. The more the files are opened up, the more we are bound to be treated to further unsavory revelations. Sometimes I think they should just burn all that crap in a field in Ukraine somewhere and forget about it. Those files are like one last insult from the low, dishonest century just past, still reaching out from the grave to muddy the waters of the present.

* * *

The case of Kapuscinski is particularly intriguing. One of the more intrepid journalists of the 20th century, Kapuscinski spent a lot of time in forgotten or never-even-known-in-the-first-place towns in Africa, Latin America, and the former Soviet Empire. He wrote straight journalism for the Polish Press Agency, but his most important works were a blend of storytelling, prose poetry, and historical narrative that attempted to capture something more fundamental about the places and people he experienced. Works like *The Emperor* (a narrative of the last days of Haile Selassie's court) and *Shah of Shahs* (about the downfall of Mohammad Reza Pahlavi) were more than reporting, they were about the soul of a time and place.

Recently, Kapuscinski died. But he left to us a posthumous publication called *Travels with Herodotus*. In the book, Kapuscinski explains that he had the writings of Herodotus — the ancient Greek writer often referred to as "The Father of History" — as a constant companion during his travels and that the stories Herodotus tells were a touchstone for his impressions of the modern world. Indeed, Kapuscinski all but names himself as the modern incarnation of Herodotus. This is notable in reference to Kapuscinski because there was another name given to Herodotus, an accusation that goes all the way back to his near contemporary, Thucydides. The dig is that Herodotus is "The Father of Lies." Indeed, in the account of the Peloponnesian War, Thucydides accuses Herodotus (though without explicitly naming him) of writing down "any story that comes his way" and of being less than devoted to the cause of truth.

That same accusation has dogged Kapuscinski. Even before the revelations about his work for SB came to light, Kapuscinski had been taken to task repeatedly for presenting works that seemed to blur the boundary between journalism and fiction while helping themselves to the authority of the former. He was accused of being a liar.

So it's tempting to see the Herodotus book as Kapuscinski's response. If so, he is saying, in essence, "I am a liar. And so what?" And even more audaciously, he also seems to be claiming, "I am a liar in the service of something greater than truth, if you conceive of truth merely as accuracy in relation to the 'facts.'" There's a passage from *Travels with Herodotus* that cuts right to the heart of this claim. Kapuscinski is describing how he came to like and admire Herodotus in reading him. He says,

> It was an affinity with a human being whom I did not know personally, yet who charmed me by the manner of his relationships with others, by his way of being, by how, whenever he appeared, he instantly became the nucleus, or the mortar, of human community, putting it together, bringing it into being.

The emphasis in those pages is on the figure of the storyteller and his role as the "nucleus of human community," the one responsible for "bringing it into being." And it is hard not to think that Kapuscinski sees himself that way, as somehow responsible for the unity and possibility of human community itself. In those same pages Kapuscinski speaks of Herodotus, and thereby himself, as "someone unique and irreplaceable, one who could interpret the world and guide his fellows through it." His defense of himself as a writer (and as a potential liar) revolves around this conception of himself as being beyond truth and lies. Kapuscinski saw himself, it seems, as a kind of guarantor of the possibility of communication in the first place, as at the very root of the process by which we even have the capacity to lie or to tell the truth. He saw himself as a source, and the source cannot be judged in the same way that other things can.

I'll admit that I came to writing about Kapuscinski with the intention of defending him, praising him. I think his writings are unique and that they traverse a ground between fiction and nonfiction that tells us something important about who we are. I think he is right that we need historians who are also storytellers, who understand that mode of human communication. But the more I've looked over those passages the more I think it is too complicated for simple praise or blame. If I'm right that Kapuscinski is defending himself in these pages, then it is an odd and troubling defense. It has the flavor of grandiosity to the point of feeling desperate, creepy. I don't know if it is a healthy thing to think of yourself as someone tasked with interpreting the world and guiding everyone else through it, as the nucleus of human community.

In the beginning of *Travels with Herodotus*, Kapuscinski talks about his youth and the beginning of his fascination with Herodotus. It arose out of the ashes of a nation and a community utterly destroyed. He writes, "We were children of war. High schools were closed during the war years and although in the larger cities clandestine classes were occasionally convened, here, in this lecture hall, sat mostly boys and girls from remote villages and small towns, ill read, uneducated. It was 1951." 1951 in Poland is a big deal. It is the dazed landscape of civilization in ruins.

Like everyone who emerged from that experience, Kapuscinski will always be defined by that destruction and its aftermath and by the choices and compromises he had to make in its wake. He wrote some beautiful books, but the more we look back at those books the more we have to see them as strange treasures. Kapuscinski constructed for himself an identity as a savior and interpreter and protector of human community. He saw himself as a mythical hero of the human story. That made him great, but great in the way that leaves an odd taste in the mouth. Kapuscinski was willing to do almost anything to tell his story. But that isn't necessarily a good thing. If nothing else, it reminds us just how long are the arms of Western civilization's traumas.

By Morgan Meis
6 August 2007

Osama bin Laden

(1957 – 2011)

The scariest thing about Osama bin Laden was his quietness and his calm. He spoke softly. His face was soft, too. His gestures were never harsh or abrupt. He seemed to be a gentle man. Osama bin Laden was, of course, an extremely violent man. He was so obsessed with violence that, at times, it seemed the purpose of al-Qaeda was violence for violence's sake. I suspect (though cannot prove) that his obsession with violence stemmed from an overdeveloped sense of vengeance and punishment. He said it himself, one time. He explained that his experience of watching Israel invade Lebanon in 1982 with the help of the American 6th Fleet changed him.

> In these tough moments, many things raged inside me that are hard to describe, but they resulted in a strong feeling against injustice and a strong determination to punish the unjust. While I was looking at these destroyed towers in Lebanon, it sparked in my mind that the tyrant should be punished with the same and that we should destroy towers in America, so that it tastes what we taste and would be deterred from killing our children and women.

We will never exactly know what feelings raged inside the man: The strong perception of injustice does different things to different people. In bin Laden, it grew a terrible need to punish, a feeling that no punishment would be too strong, a passionate conviction that he was a divine tool of punishment placed upon this Earth for that purpose alone.

He put away the rage, though. He locked it up. He decided that he would be a more effective tool of punishment if he did not speak the rage inside him, did not attempt to describe it, to verbalize the rage itself. Bin Laden never ranted or raved as other men of great violence do. The speeches of Adolf Hitler are always a touching point. Hitler would whip himself into a frenzy as he spoke, driving himself into heights of outrage that spilled over and into the audience. The point was to unleash those demons of violence in himself and therefore let everyone listening know that they, too, could unleash those demons. Hitler wanted to sculpt a German public that was comfortable with the angry and dark passions of violence. He wanted them to feel that rage was appropriate and that the actions resulting from rage were the natural next step. Hitler never found it difficult to express his rage. He gloried in expressing it. He lived to express it. He became one of the acknowledged masters of expressing rage.

Osama bin Laden went the opposite route. His was the calm and deliberate side of violence. But it was fearsome. I often like to pretend — for my own sense of sanity and well-being — that it takes a great disruption of a man's normal feelings and emotions to get him to the point of killing. I like to pretend that great violence cannot be acted out within a state of dispassion. At least, then, we would always know when it was coming. We would witness the fit of rage and be prepared for the forth-coming storm of violence. The way the 9/11 attackers spent their lives as everyday members of American society in the months leading up to that day, the way they boarded the planes as normal men, the way they flew the planes deliberately into those towers — they are an outgrowth of the calm, detached violence that bin Laden personified.

If nothing else, the life of Osama bin Laden was a testimony to the varieties of violence that can be encountered within the human being. He discovered a ruthlessness where it was least expected. He discovered that a capacity for killing could be found within a state of repose, that anger — cooled and pushed deep into the recesses of the soul — could be a terrifying weapon precisely because it was so cold. He discovered that gentle speech and a warm smile could be a vehicle for punishment and a tool for violence. It is a lesson, I suppose, in human capacity.

* * *

The most surprising thing about the death of Osama bin Laden was his funeral. Islamic law declares that a person must be buried within 24 hours of death. "We are ensuring that it is handled in accordance with Islamic practice and tradition," *Time* reported a U.S. official as saying. "This is something that we take very seriously. And so therefore, this is being handled in an appropriate manner."

Bin Laden was buried at sea, presumably so that there will be no burial site, no country that owns him, no place on Earth that can be associated with him ever after. The sea gets him, being the only place capacious enough to take on the burden. There is dignity in having done it this way. Not dignity for him, but dignity for us. It is understandable that people want to celebrate the death of a man who scared us, who was the author of a traumatizing act of violence, who plotted the deaths of thousands and dreamed of the deaths of thousands upon thousands more. But I am not sure that celebrating death ever does anything very good for the one who celebrates.

I shuddered for the souls of the men at Saddam Hussein's execution. The footage is, now, widely available on the Internet. It was captured surreptitiously on a cell-phone video camera. Saddam is brought into a dingy room in what looks like a basement. He is bustled toward a noose and begins praying. Some of the people standing below begin to shout. They are calling out, "Muqtada," in reference to Muqtada al-Sadr, the Shia religious and political leader. Saddam says the name Muqtada back to them and then asks, "Do you call this courage?" Another person yells at Saddam to go to hell. He replies, "The hell that is Iraq?" Then he goes back to praying. All of a sudden, the trap door beneath Saddam opens and he plummets. He is gone. It is impossible to watch that footage without feeling that Saddam stole his dignity back in those final moments. The people in the room gave Saddam the opportunity to do it. They gave him a moment to be the honorable one in death. It lessened those men, those witnesses. They became small in the face of the ultimate thing, the death of a human being.

The last few days have seen a lot of talk about whether or not it is appropriate to celebrate the killing of Osama bin Laden. I would phrase the question in a different way. What does it do to one human being to celebrate the killing of another human being, whatever the circumstances? What happens inside you, how does it make you feel? Is that something you want to feel? Is it a way you want to be? I think of the witnesses at Saddam Hussein's funeral, the ones who cried out. I imagine them walking out into the sunlight of the bright day outside and feeling exposed, thinned out, cheated of the euphoria they had hoped to feel. Maybe they wished, in retrospect, that they would have had the strength to stay silent and serious for the final act of a long tragedy in which no one emerged unscathed.

The gently smiling face of Osama bin Laden will be an image that stays with us for a long time, anyway. It was proper to let go of it, down into the ocean's depths. It will be an accomplishment just to let it go.

By Morgan Meis
4 May 2011

Charlton Heston

(1923 – 2008)

As the story goes, Cecil B. DeMille chose Charlton Heston to play Moses in his epic *The Ten Commandments* because Heston looked a hell of a lot like the Moses of Michelangelo's famous statue. Apocryphal or not, I believe it. It had to have been an awesome experience being approached by a young Charlton Heston. It had to have been like running into a statue — rock-hewn, solid, but supple all the same. He does look like that statue.

As a child I was transfixed by the presence of him, by the way he towers over things in that movie. I remember watching it with my sister more than once. She was barely more than a toddler, even less able than I was to expend much attention on a feature film. But Mr. Heston nailed her to a spot on the floor. He had something, some power to do that to us.

I recognize that the film is dangerously close to being kitsch. One need only glance at a picture of Edward G. Robinson as the Israelite apostate Dathan to get a sense of the absurdity of DeMille's spectacle. Edward G. Robinson was born to wear a three-piece suit, not dance around in leather jerkin with an ashtray on his head. But Heston saved it, somehow, just with the presence he manages to get into the camera and onto the screen.

That's the irony of the movie, I suppose. Cecil B. DeMille was famous for, among other things, throwing actors around like so many buzzing flies filling up the space of his filmic tableaux. He didn't count actors by talent so much as by sheer numerical quantity. If a good movie takes 50 actors, he seems to have surmised, a really great one will take 5000.

In *The Ten Commandments* DeMille wanted to tell "the greatest story ever told." He tossed the actors out in handfuls and piled on the sets as if he himself could speak the word to material things, thus making them be. But the movie is dated. The techniques, from the acting to the camera work, are trapped in a pathetic no man's land between the era of early filmmaking from which DeMille was spawned and the technologies and sensibilities of another generation. The only one who could hold it together was one of the cogs in the machine, a granite-faced man who looked like a statue become flesh. Heston is what is great about *The Ten Commandments*, not Cecil B. DeMille. DeMille's next move, right after the movie was finished, was to die.

Now Charlton Heston is just as dead as DeMille. The sad part about it is that, like DeMille, he lingered too long past his time. He was a guest on *Saturday Night Live* in 1993. I remember watching the episode in a sustained cringe. Some of the sketches may even have been funny. But it was clear that he didn't really know why they were funny. He wasn't understanding the world around him anymore. He had the lost look of a grandparent confronted with something a little too new, a little too far past the framework of reference. It is analogous to the difference between his youthful and bold defense of the Civil Rights Movement in the early '60s and his pitiful trumpeting of stale NRA rhetoric in old age.

That is a troubling thought. One benefit of getting old, we like to imagine, is the benefit of gaining wisdom. Experience is supposed to confer a kind of wizened capacity for judgment. You gain a sense not just for how things seem to work in the moment, but also for how they really work, how they've always worked. But that isn't how it often goes. Cecil B. DeMille became a clown. Charlton Heston became a damn fool.

Life for them, real life, did not span the entirety of their lived existence. It spanned a few short decades when they were both in the world and of the world. That is what made them big. You could call it the bigness of immanence. And yet that vital immanence drifts away as capriciously as it drifts in. Charlton Heston was living in this world during the last few decades of his life, but not really. In fact, he had been shunted off to its periphery, a baffled old man. Our only solace is that it makes his moment of immanence all the more luminous. Not many men could trade their flesh against the stone of Michelangelo's statue. At least we have to give the old man that.

By Morgan Meis
8 April 2008

Mary Ellen Mark

(1940 – 2015)

In a photograph titled "Ward 81," a woman sits on a bed. She is young, a teenager. She sits cross-legged and wears her clothes and hair like a teenager would. The wall behind this teenage girl is covered in pictures. The pictures, magazine cutouts, are taped to the wall and some of the edges have been carefully rounded with scissors. There are pictures of animals and a picture of a tree. Below a picture of the *Mona Lisa* the name BRENDA is written in marker. In this room that could belong to any teenager, the walls are strangely close. The bed is pushed up to the radiator and the metal headboard is too white and plain. The young woman's eyes are blank; one eye tilts toward her nose. The woman's left arm is outstretched and bears the evidence of self-inflicted wounds. On the wall above the radiator, also written in marker, are the words, "I wish to die."

This photograph was taken by Mary Ellen Mark, who died on May 25. Mark was adamant that her work be called documentary photography. "I'm a documentary photographer," she told *Bomb* magazine in 1989. "That's what I've always wanted to be; that's where my heart and soul is." The word "document," when applied to photographs, conveys the sense of proof, evidence, testimony. A document is an affirmation of the subject being documented, proof of that subject's existence, if nothing else. A documentary photograph says, "Here is the person that existed when this photograph was taken."

Mary Ellen Mark liked to photograph people who dwelled on society's fringes: street kids, prostitutes, junkies, the homeless, women who were mentally ill (like the women who lived within the confines of Ward 81)—the survivors, the "unlucky ones." Every one of her photographs could have held the same caption:

"I exist." Mary Ellen Mark said her main interest was reality. Documenting the marginal and the lost was, for Mark, to show the world as it really is. Mark wanted to bring her subjects out of the shadows, to make their existence real.

The Foreword of Mark's book of photographs of the women of Ward 81 (*Ward 81*) is a story by Milos Foreman:

> I once heard a story about two women in a small town in Czechoslovakia. At the end of World War II ... each woman took to the streets in euphoria and attacked the retreating German tanks, yelling abuse and throwing stones. The Germans fired on the first woman and killed her instantly. The second woman, for reasons unknown, was ignored by the fleeing army. Screaming hysterically, she was led away by her compatriots and taken to a mental institution ...
>
> The woman who had been killed became a hero. Her photograph made the front pages of the newspapers ... The woman who had been ignored spent five years in a mental institution. As far as I know no one ever bothered to photograph her.

In Mary Ellen Mark's photographs, the women of Ward 81 cannot be ignored. Each subject's presence fills the frame. But if you look close enough, you will see the presence of Mary Ellen Mark there, too. Mark didn't believe in the total objectivity of a portrait, in which the photographer is supposedly absent. A subject is always aware of the person taking the picture, Mark would say. You can sense the presence of the photographer in the angle of a photo, and in the posing of the subject. Sometimes, you can actually see the photographer's image reflected in her subject's gaze.

Mary Ellen Mark lived with her subjects, figuratively and often actually. A former head cheerleader from the suburbs of Philadelphia, Mark always felt an affinity for faraway lands and outliers. She wanted to travel, go places, see the world's truth. In the late '70s, Mark spent months lingering around cafes and brothels for her series *Falkland Road: Prostitutes of Bombay*, striking up conversations, dodging insults, until "slowly, very slowly," Mark once wrote, "I began to make friends." In 1976, Mark confined herself to the Oregon State Hospital for 36 days in what was then the state's only a maximum-security asylum for women: Ward 81. "I think I was interested because my father had several nervous breakdowns and was hospitalized several times," she told *The New York Times* years later. Or maybe, she said, it was the fascinating class trip to a mental hospital she had taken in the third grade. "For years I'd planned to go live in a mental hospital," she said. "I wanted to see if I could feel something of what it was like to be set aside from society."

Mary Ellen Mark photographed monsters. They were not monsters in the beastly or demonic sense but rather, in the way Mary Shelley conceived her monster in *Frankenstein*, creatures both inside and outside humanity. The Latin word "monstrar," just like the word "docere" (from which "document" comes) means "to show." The abnormality of the monster is itself a form of proof, a window onto reality. Mary Ellen Mark photographed monsters of all sorts but she was especially interested in women: autistic women, elderly women, women in the circus, women on the street, women who have been institutionalized for madness, women who have lost limbs to leprosy, homeless girls, girls with cancer, prostitutes. Even her photographs of Mother Teresa put the nun in the same context as the sick and poor in her care. In Mark's photos, Teresa was just another a woman living at the extreme outer limits of civilization.

Mary Ellen Mark's women are never, at first glance, what they seem. Often, their monstrosities are nearly invisible. Mark's genius was to capture the subtlety of a woman's monstrosity: the errant scar, the odd slump of a body, the too-happy smile, the worldly-wise and cynical stare. On a Fulbright scholarship in 1965, Mark took a photo she later called *Beautiful Emine posing,*

Trabzon, Turkey, 1965. Mark considered it her first real picture. In *Beautiful Emine posing*, a lovely young girl wears a frilly dress and a big bow in her hair. Emine looks at the camera straight on, two fingers on her right cheek, two hands on her thigh. She knows that she is beautiful. But Emine's hair is just a little too messy and her white shoes are dirty. On a man, there is nothing scandalous about dirty shoe. On a woman, a dirty shoe is a story. Spending time with the people living in Ward 81, Mary Ellen Mark didn't find that much difference between the inmates' behavior and her own. "Maybe they were too sensitive," she said, "and couldn't cope." Even a woman's sensitivity, Mark was saying, could be a declaration of her freakishness.

In *Frankenstein*, the monster wants nothing more than to be a part of humanity. Denied this right, he asks his maker for just one thing: another monster with whom to share his monstrous life. This desire to belong is once again "proof." Belonging connects us to reality, becomes the evidence that we are alive. Looked at like this, there is not much difference between the desire to be head cheerleader and the desire to escape to the streets. There is the same battle with loneliness, the same longing to have a home. Though Mark's subjects were marginalized from mainstream society, they always seemed to find each other. The prostitutes of Bombay, the street kids, and the women of Ward 81 made little communities among themselves. The monstrosities that held these people apart from the mainstream, from their families – sometimes from themselves – connected them to kindred spirits. In the text for *Ward 81*, the writer Karen Folger Jacobs (who confined herself along with Mark) wrote of an inmate named Mary. One day, the staff decided to move Mary to an unlocked ward, separating Mary from her best friend Grace. "There's only one thing that's beautiful on 81," Mary told Mark and Jacobs, referring to her separation from Grace. "It's not the ward itself. It's the love, the friendship, the unity of it all, the blessedness we share with each other. We're patient with each other, waiting to be free together."

Mary Ellen Mark's project has been repeatedly compared to predecessor Diane Arbus (Mark disliked the connection). Arbus, too, was attracted to monsters, and saw her own monstrosity in the subjects she photographed. Mark felt her approach, however, was ultimately different than that of Arbus; she called Arbus a distant "observer" of marginal people. Arbus was, in a sense, jealous of the people she photographed: the giants, the twins, the young men in curlers. These people were more "real" than everyone else. Arbus, who was raised in an atmosphere of privilege she resented, once said, "Most people go through life dreading they'll have a traumatic experience. Freaks were born with their trauma. They've already passed their test in life. They're aristocrats." Arbus admired her subjects but she could not connect her own monstrousness to theirs, nor seemingly, to anyone's, ending her life in a bathtub at the age of 48. Arbus' monsters were monsters of separation.

Mark had a great respect for her subjects' monstrosities, too, but she didn't linger on them. Rather, Mark's photographs aimed to move through difference in order to access an underlying humanity. This is why it wasn't enough for Mary Ellen Mark to document the lives of mental patients and prostitutes "objectively." She had to immerse herself in these lives, be frightened with them, know them. "It's amazing," she once told *Vanity Fair*, "how intimate you can get even when you go into someone's life only for a few days."

In 1999, Aperture published a collection of Mary Ellen Mark's photographs called *American Odyssey, 1963-1999*. The book starts with a Maya Angelou poem. The poem is called "Human Family"; it begins and ends like this:

I note the obvious differences
in the human family.
Some of us are serious,

some thrive on comedy.

Some declare their lives are lived
as true profundity,
and others claim they really live
the real reality.
…
I note the obvious differences
between each sort and type,
but we are more alike, my friends,
than we are unalike.

We are more alike, my friends,
than we are unalike.

We are more alike, my friends,
than we are unalike.

In this collection of photographs, among the retired rodeo
workers and the teenage mothers and the burned-out kids along
the Jersey shore, are Idaho housewives in Aryan Nations
costumes, and white supremacist teenagers, and enthusiastic
participants of a KKK rally pulling up a huge cross in the hills of
Tennessee at night. Mark never stopped searching the corners of
life, seeking out the shunned. Flipping through the photographs
of Mary Ellen Mark, you are bound to be confronted by a human
being you have never seen before, and perhaps do not wish to
see. While many of her subjects might garner a viewer's
sympathy, sympathy was never Mark's goal. It was not pity Mark
was trying to capture in her work but, once again, reality. The
photographs of white supremacists are shot with the same sensitivity and silence with which Mark shot all her subjects, the same
acknowledgment of a common humanity. These people, too, live
in society's shadows, are a community of monsters wanting to

belong. "I exist," the people in these photographs say. "We are more alike, my friends, than we are unalike."

By Stefany Anne Golberg
8 June 2015

Robert Rauschenberg

(1925 – 2008)

Robert Rauschenberg died last week. That makes it, I suppose, the end of an era. There's no question that Rauschenberg changed art — the way it's practiced, the way it is received, the things you can do and still call it art. Contemporary art is Rauschenbergian. Even Warhol, the other father of contemporary art, owes the man a massive debt.

The simplest way to explain what Rauschenberg did is to say that he made the canvas three-dimensional and worldly. Or to put it another way, he thought of the canvas as something you could walk inside and inhabit. There's a famous quote that has come to define Rauschenberg's practice. It goes, "I operate in the gap between art and life."

There's a piece by Robert Rauschenberg that now lives at the MoMA. It's called *Bed* (1955). It isn't exactly a painting and it isn't exactly a bed. There are bed elements — an actual sheet, a pillow, a quilt. Rumor has it that these bed elements were once the very things that Rauschenberg slept on. But there are painting elements as well. First of all, it is framed and up on the wall. Secondly, there's the paint, smeared and splattered mostly around the top half of the work.

Arthur Danto, the art critic for *The Nation*, makes an insightful point about these early works (Rauschenberg called them "Combines"). He notes that Rauschenberg felt a need to arrange a bunch of objects and then to throw paint over them. It is as if he is still under the thrall of paint, convinced that it is the paint itself that is making the difference between art and not-art. But he's also trying to cure himself, and by extension the art world dominated by painterly Modernism, of this addiction. Slowly he realized that he didn't need the paint at all. He became indifferent to its authority. Even when he came back to paint and painting throughout his career, he did so as a free man.

In the end, I don't think Rauschenberg's work can be understood outside the context of the High Modernism from which it emerged. Rauschenberg was operating in a milieu dominated by the formal problems of space, line, color, surface. And even if the Abstract Expressionists believed that they were expressing deep and intense feelings with their work, they took it for granted that those feelings, when expressed in art, ought to be purified of every particular. It was feeling as such, not this or that feeling.

Rauschenberg's *Bed* is startling because of its actual bedness. The quilt is a real quilt, it has been slept with, it still has the residue of specific nights, specific experiences. It has meaning not because it tells us something about beds as such. It doesn't reduce the bed to its abstract rectangular form or deconstruct it into a series of angles. Instead, it wants to be that very bed that it is, to tell us something about one bed that existed in a unique place and time. We should also mention that *Bed* is funny. It's amusing that *Bed* is, in some basic way, just a bed. It is the reverse joke of Magritte's painting of a pipe that declares "This is not a pipe."

Rauschenberg's innovation was to grab actual pieces of the real world in order to keep hold of the particularity, and the meaning inherent within that particularity, that he felt was missing from so much of the art of his time. By grabbing chunks of the real world he was borrowing the associations, thoughts, memories, and references that would inevitably come along with them. He once said, "I think a painting is more like the real world if it's made out of the real world." And then he tossed those elements of the real world around and mixed them up and played with them. That is the freedom of the aesthetic "gap" between art and life that he was messing about in. He simply wasn't interested in whether the arrangement of things is pleasing or beautiful in terms of the balance between form and material. He was interested in the way that the meaning which clings to objects of the world gets shifted and transformed when they are taken up into the aesthetic dimension.

The central intuition behind Rauschenberg's art is thus that the world is interesting enough just as we find it. Getting too far away from that doesn't get you deeper insight or deeper truth, it just takes you farther away. Meaning, for Rauschenberg, was always contained in the things closest to us, literally, the stuff around you in your room. But he couldn't leave all the things, the bric-a-brac of daily existence, well enough alone either. Thus the "gap" between art and life. He wanted to bring the objects of the world closer to art in order to make them weird and fascinating, and he wanted to bring art closer to the things of the world in order to make it more real. It is utterly pointless to debate whether Rauschenberg's accomplishment was a "good" or "bad" thing for art. More essentially, it was a necessary thing. It leapt over the cul-de-sac of High Modernism and pointed ahead to something new. Art followed him because he provided real answers. Alas, those answers, like Rauschenberg, are finite and will give way to different problems and still different answers. I'm sure Bob wouldn't have had it any other way.

By Morgan Meis
21 May 2008

Thomas Kinkade

(1958 – 2012)

I was surprised to read that Thomas Kinkade, "Painter of Light," had died at age 54. It seems only yesterday I was in the Thomas Kinkade Gallery at the Fashion Show Mall in Las Vegas, ambling through fantastically homey landscapes in pink and blue pastels. Quaint brick houses with sloping straw rooftops and fresh green lawns dotted with lazy horses under a perfect blue sky. A yellow-brick road dappled with autumn sun. A lighthouse standing sentry beneath a splash of coastline. A stone house frosted in snow by a lightly frozen river, and standing by the river, in a ring of luminescence, two deer. All the windows in all the houses in all the landscapes have the glow of a magical hearth, as if lit by heaven itself. Everything in Las Vegas glows but not like Kinkade's paintings. The light in Las Vegas is temporary and utilitarian in its showiness. There is nothing in its glow that feels so everlasting as the light of Kinkade, except the sunset over the valley.

Obituaries reported that 1 in 20 American homes displays a work of Thomas Kinkade. I read that Thomas Kinkade was (and still is) the most successful artist in all America. This news is at first surprising, and then not surprising at all. What American artist would be his rival? There are hundreds of Thomas Kinkade shops selling paintings of light across the country (not to mention in the U.K., Canada, Malaysia, Ireland, Russia…). Certainly, no other American painter has hundreds of shops of their paintings — most don't even have one. Many have argued that there are American artists more deserving of shops than Kinkade, real artists who wouldn't accept Kinkade's level of popularity even if it were offered. Yet America loves Thomas Kinkade — loves to love him or loves to hate him — and now that Kinkade is dead, love-hate him all the more.

Thomas Kinkade is the "Painter of Light." Kinkade, who became a born-again Christian in the 1980s, wanted to lift people up with his art, to take them out of the darkness. He felt strongly that painting could achieve this and felt just as strongly that the contemporary fine-art world had failed in this project. "My mission as an artist," Kinkade wrote on his website, "is to capture those special moments in life adorned with beauty and light. I work to create images that project a serene simplicity that can be appreciated and enjoyed by everyone. That's what I mean by sharing the light." Art, for Kinkade, was not meant to criticize society, and shouldn't be reserved for an educated few. Painting was an "inspirational tool," an alternative to the ugliness of the nightly news. "People who put my paintings on their walls," he once told *The New York Times*, "are putting their values on their walls: faith, family, home, a simpler way of living, the beauty of nature, quiet, tranquility, peace, joy, hope."

It's a big claim, calling yourself a painter of light. Taking on the challenge of light is no anodyne endeavor. To allow light into a painting, one must capture it, this element that is so elusive, both ephemeral and earthly, both infinite and finite. Many painters throughout history chose to sidestep the problem of light, perhaps including an occasional representative of light instead — a halo, a sun god. There were those brave few who took on light almost as their primary task. Rembrandt; the pre-Raphaelites; the Impressionists, who used people and landscapes as vehicles for the expression of light; J.M.W. Turner, whose use of light so moved the critic John Ruskin that the latter was compelled to write a prose-poem in praise of it:

There is the motion, the actual wave and radiation of the darted beam: not the dull universal daylight, which falls on the landscape without life, or direction, or speculation, equal on all things and dead on all things; but the breathing, animated, exulting light, which feels, and receives, and rejoices, and acts ...which seeks, and finds, and loses again... glowing, or flashing, or scintillating, according to what it strikes; or, in its holier moods, absorbing and enfolding all things in the deep fulness of its repose, and then again losing itself in bewilderment, and doubt, and dimness...

As Adam Kirsch once wrote, Turner and Ruskin were both Romantics, "striving after an infinity that art can barely contain." Painting light is just this: the revelation of an unsolvable mystery, the attempt to frame a barely containable infinity. Bewilderment, doubt. Dimness.

Light has almost always, in Western painting, anyway, been used to convey a sense of transcendence, whether in religious iconography or natural landscape. Come the 20th century, however, and light suddenly disappears behind a flat layer of two-dimensional shapes and splotches. Modernism was greatly concerned with universals, even with the sacred, but not specifically with how light expresses them. You could say that Modernism was a letting-go of the light. Then, in the 1960s, light made a comeback, in the form of light sculpture and light environments. Dan Flavin created his sculptures with generic mass-produced light fixtures, like the kind you would find at the DMV. But rather than lifting you up, Flavin hoped that, when you walked into one of his environments, you would find the experience to be just as banal as the DMV. "My icons differ from a Byzantine Christ held in majesty," Flavin once wrote in a record book, "they are dumb — anonymous and inglorious. They are as mute and indistinguished as the run of our architecture. My icons do not raise up the blessed savior in elaborate cathedrals. They are constructed concentrations celebrating barren rooms. They bring a limited light." Just as natural light can be used to lift people up artificially, Flavin was saying, so can artificial light be used as the denial of transcendence.

Flavin's iconoclastic approach to light is almost the mirror opposite of Thomas Kinkade's. It is true that the mass accessibility of Kinkade's paintings and their cozy, unpretentious themes made Thomas Kinkade a very rich man. But his accessibility cannot be disentangled from his painting philosophy. Accessibility and pretty colors were crucial for conveying Kinkade's idea of a palpable, personal illumination. Kinkade's paintings are, in this way, a bit like the Gideon's Bible. Kinkade's light is an everywhere, anytime transcendence.

As Kinkade himself said, light is optimism — and optimism is always a mix of hope and fantasy, of the natural and supernatural. A thatched-roof house in a grove that recalls a memory of a perfectly nameless country town is also reminiscent of a hobbit house from *The Lord of the Rings*. A fawn standing in a flowerbed by a stream looks to an impossible rainbow that juts from a cliff, and the deer also happens to be Bambi. This unapologetically sincere optimism is an easy target. There is something childish, even ludicrous, about optimism. For this reason, Kinkade's light is melancholy, too. At the Fashion Show Mall in Las Vegas last year, I was reminded of something Robert Walser once wrote about the easy delights of Berlin's Tiergarten. It was like a painted picture, he wrote, "then like a dream, then like a circuitous, agreeable kiss ... [O]ne is lightly, comprehensibly enticed to gaze and linger." *A Circuitous, Agreeable Kiss* might be the name for any one of Thomas Kinkade's paintings, for this title conveys well the sense of longing and melancholy that stimulates both Kinkade's critics and fans.

Thomas Kinkade has been likened to Norman Rockwell, that other American populist who painted scenes of a happier America in a bygone age. Like Rockwell, some have said, Kinkade attracted Americans not so much with hope but with nostalgia, the sweet sorrow of loss. Yet Kinkade's paintings are not nostalgic; they are simply unreal. If anything, they depict an America that has never existed, and will never exist. It is the fantasy, I think, that makes them attractive.

I have often wondered that there are rarely people in Thomas Kinkade's paintings (his Disney paintings being an exception, though they are peopled by fictional characters). Kinkade said he kept his scenes empty so that people could project themselves into the paintings. To me, these empty landscapes of Kinkade feel more haunted than fantastic, as if the little house on the hill had to be suddenly and inexplicably vacated, its inhabitants not given even enough time to turn off the lights and stifle the fire in the hearth.

By Stefany Anne Golberg
12 April 2012

Roman Opalka

(1931 – 2011)

In 1965, while waiting in a cafe, Roman Opalka decided he would paint time. He didn't paint the counters of time — clocks and watches and calendars and such. He didn't paint people waiting for the bus or racing to the finish line. Roman Opalka painted time itself. He called this project, his life's work, "OPALKA 1965 / 1 – ∞." The title might be read as this: "(Roman) Opalka (the artist, begins in) 1965 (painting numbers from) one to infinity."

Having decided to paint time, the French-Polish conceptual artist went to his Warsaw studio and prepared a canvas. He sat before it. His hand trembled. He knew that once he started this immense project, he could never go back. Armed with a size-0 brush and still shaking, Opalka painted a little white "1" on the upper left-hand corner of a gray canvas. He then made his way horizontally across the canvas, number by number — 2...3...4...5 — until he had a row of numbers, then two rows of numbers, then three. When Opalka ran out of room, when the last number was painted in the bottom right-hand corner, he stopped. Later, the artist made another painting, and then another, each one picking up numerically where the last painting left off. He called the paintings "Details." The canvas was always the same size: 196 centimeters by 135 centimeters. The numbers were always painted in white. When Opalka made a Detail, he recorded himself speaking the numbers as he painted. When a painting session was finished, Opalka would take a photograph of his face in front of his work, the numbers stopping when he did. Opalka devoted himself to this project alone, the project of painting time. "All my work is a single thing," he once wrote, "the description from number one to infinity."

Opalka painted millions of numbers for more than 45 years,

stroke by stroke, and took hundreds of self-portraits: same lighting, same position, same purpose. You would think that this formality would make Opalka's paintings uniform, cold. But a single Detail is dizzying to behold. At first glance you can't really see that you are looking at numbers. Because Opalka was committed to the hand-painted gesture, the digits are all uneven, both in size and weight. Before you can get a good look at the content, Opalka's paintings feel as though they are moving around as the numbers get heavier and lighter, like the disappearing cloud of dust that follows the Roadrunner as he zips offscreen.

Roman Opalka painted time and he painted it moving forward: 1, 2, 3, and on... If Opalka painted time counting backward, his project would have still moved in the direction of infinity. But even though Roman Opalka painted toward infinity, he wasn't trying to paint infinity itself. Opalka painted time moving forward because Opalka was painting death. "Time as we live it and as we create it," Opalka wrote, "embodies our progressive disappearance; we are at the same time alive and in the face of death — that is the mystery of all living beings." The very fact of our living is to embody our own disappearance. At first, the Details were painted on a dark background, the numbers in white. But in 1972, Opalka began lightening the background of each canvas by one percent. In 2008, the artist started painting white on white, calling the color *blanc mérité* (well-earned white). As the numbers he painted grew in size, as the canvases grew lighter, Opalka's face — documented before a Detail at the end of each work session — grew lighter, too. His face lost structure, his hair grew whiter. In a symbolic way, to look at the Details is to watch Opalka die. Opalka's concern with the infinite future, with death, is the great concern of us all. Which is why the infinity in front of one's life looms much larger than the infinity behind, for Opalka and for us. We are beings toward death, disappearing with each breath in the face of a progression of time that is utterly indifferent to us.

All of this makes Opalka's work sound mortifyingly bleak. Only a person this simultaneously Polish and French, you are thinking, could concoct for himself such a godforsaken, death-obsessed life project. When Opalka began "OPALKA 1965 / 1 – ∞," he wasn't interested in the mystical or "esoteric" aspect of numbers. "I wanted to be as rational a painter as I possibly could," he wrote. Opalka wanted the act of painting numbers to be utterly methodical, woven into his daily practice as completely as eating or sleeping. But something happened to Opalka as he continued his project over the years; he "chanced upon a mysterious potential in the logic of numbers." Namely, he stopped thinking about the slow, bleak, methodical progression of time and realized that, as he painted, he felt himself to be inside a continuum of time, "the dynamic unity of a spacetime structure." Time, as he painted, was not just moving forward but all around him. And as it did, Opalka realized that painting time wasn't just documenting his life; it *was* his life. Speaking in a television interview for France 3 in 1994, Opalka said:

> I took my body, my length, my existence as I have often said, as a sort of pictorial sacrifice and the essence, the embodiment of this procedure, creates a work much the same as we all create works with our lives. Every time that I add a number, everything changes. It is a sort of journey, if you will, where the steps are conscious each and every time, each step adds to the others, the weight of the duration of all these steps that you have lived. I even use death as a tool for a work. To finish, in order to complete a work, I use death as a tool.

In the sentence "Roman Opalka painted time," the word "painted" is just as important as "time." Opalka was an artist. He felt it wasn't enough to just think about time; he had to create something out of it, "define" it. Opalka painted time slouching toward infinity but what he painted was the condition of finitude. Opalka knew that, even as beings toward death, our real obsession is not death but life. It is living with the knowledge of death, which always happens in the future, that makes it hard to experience our lives as something happening now. We are always looking toward this most future of future events. Possessing both the knowledge that we are alive and the knowledge that we will die can make us feel part-dead. But Roman Opalka thought that if you really went all-in with time, you could really experience living in the moment. I would guess that, as Opalka painted time, he forgot about infinity. He just painted. Painted and painted and painted, until what started as a project about man's disappearance in the face of time became the expression of a life as it was lived. "All my work is a single thing, the description from one to infinity," Roman Opalka said. "A single thing, a single life."

Roman Opalka made time his own. It's a cliché that all artists are hounded by impermanence, and create with the goal that their art will outlive them. But imagining the future of his art did not interest Opalka, which is why he created an artwork with no end. What mattered most to Opalka was that he paint time today, that he create today, that he live today. Painting infinity now kept Opalka alive. Opalka knew that, in painting time so diligently, so methodically, for decades, he had sacrificed a part of himself to it. But in embracing time, rather than fighting it, or ignoring it, Opalka was able to use his own life, and the knowledge of his own death, as tools for creation.

* * *

In his book on infinity, *Everything and More*, David Foster Wallace discussed the weirdness of concepts, of the human mind's ability to "conceive of things that we cannot, strictly speaking, conceive of." Omnipotence was a good example of this. As soon as any schoolboy learns the concept of omnipotence, Wallace wrote, he immediately starts asking questions like, "Can an omnipotent being make something too heavy for him to lift?" There is a serious rift, Wallace was saying, between what we experience (really powerful guy) and what we can conceive of (all-powerful guy). And there are few occasions when this rift is more apparent than when we think about infinity and our place within it. We "know" that we will die and yet being dead is something we can never experience. Opalka's art was partly an attempt to bridge this gap between what we can conceive about time and our actual experience living in time. To say that Roman Opalka was a conceptual artist shouldn't diminish the accessibility and the emotion in his work, nor should it make his work feel pessimistic. Consciousness of time is the mystery of life, Opalka wrote. Realizing this can be a source of joy for the single reason that it is universally shared. "This essence of reality … is not only mine but can be commonly shared in our *unus mundus*." Just that we can conceive of something bigger than ourselves, and that it includes our individual existence — well, Opalka thought, it's a beautiful thing. It's what makes us human.

In artist statements and gallery brochures, "OPALKA 1965 / 1 – ∞" is usually described as a work that would be completed only when the artist died. But if you take the title seriously, "OPALKA 1965 / 1 – ∞" is never done, can never be done, and therefore can never die, even when Opalka did. "OPALKA 1965 / 1 – ∞" cannot die simply because the numbers Opalka was painting can never end. Theoretically, there is nothing to prevent the Details from being picked up and continued by another artist, and another, and another, ad infinitum. With each new artist, the Details could continue their creep toward infinity. With each new artist, the Details would change: the gestures would be different, the faces, the colors even. I happen to think that continuing the Details after Opalka's death would be a tribute to its most profound message: the boundlessness of creation. In consciousness, we understand concepts. In experience, we embody concepts. But creating occupies the space between experience and understanding. It is in creating that the infinite and the finite can feel momentarily resolved. When we are creating — creating art or babies or laws or anything — we are, as best we can, inhabiting finitude. When we create we can feel whole, present. We can inhabit the *unus mundus* and forget death for maybe, mercifully, an instant.

On August 6, Roman Opalka died. It is rumored that the final digit Opalka painted was "8."

By Stefany Anne Golberg
19 August 2011

Cy Twombly
(1928 – 2011)

In the early 1950s, Cy Twombly worked for the army as a cryptologist. That fact seems hugely significant since Twombly was one of the more elusive artists of his generation. That is what the conventional wisdom says, anyway. In this case, the conventional wisdom is probably correct.

Cy Twombly's art first acquired its distinctively elusive characteristics when he started using letters and words in his paintings. In a number of his paintings can be found the letter "e." Twombly painted his "e"s in a cursive style most of the time, drawn with a freehand nonchalance. The "e"s in Twombly's paintings often look like something you would find in the notebook of a young person first learning to write in cursive. This person is drawing the same letter over and over again in loops in the attempt to get the form of the letter right. Maybe they have learned how to make one word and they are copying that word over and over again with varying success.

Letters, in general, are meant to make up words and words are meant to make up sentences and sentences are meant to convey meaning. Breaking sentences back down into individual words and words back down into individual letters has the opposite effect. Meaning is reduced, taken apart, decomposed. Still, the letters and the words contain a lingering residue of the meaning they are meant to lead toward even if they never get there. In Twombly's paintings, the individual "e"s looping off one another across the canvas contain a lot of promise. There is something tantalizing about the fact that they might mean something after all.

Cy Twombly seems to have enjoyed his stand-alone "e"s for just that reason. He liked to meditate on them as such. He liked the potential for meaning permanently forestalled. He must have liked the way, also, that his letter-and-word-scrawled canvases were a jolt to expectations. Paintings are supposed to be of images, while writing is supposed to use words. Words go one place, images go another. But then again, can't paintings mean something? Aren't paintings supposed to be more than mere images, more than the mere copying of reality by skilled illusionists? The move to abstraction in the generation just before Twombly was meant to be the confirmation of this fact. Abstract painters made studies in line and form and color in order to drive the point home. They were exploring the forms that make up our visual perception, or the shapes and movements that underlie our experience. Painting is not about representing reality, the abstractionists said, but is about revealing reality's true nature.

When Twombly scrawled his "e"s onto the canvas, he was taking that claim very seriously. Here is something else you can look at in a painting, he was saying. You can look at the elements of language as blocks of pure meaning just like the abstract painters were doing with their studies in pure color or pure form. We get to the essences of things, Twombly was saying. The writers may use language to say things, but the painter can show language in its abstract nature as a generator of meaning. You can't really read a painting, Twombly realized, so you have to see the language found in a painting on a different register. You have to see the language in a painting as language of painting, and not as letters and words. Even poetry, which can be the purest form of language operating for its own sake, cannot do that. Maybe that is why Twombly often gravitated to the letter "e." "E" happens to be the most commonly used letter in the English alphabet, and in many other Indo-European languages as well. There were 15 "e"s, in fact, in the previous sentence. When Georges Perec, the great Oulipian writer, wanted to set himself the most difficult formal constraint within which to write a novel, he finally came up with the idea of writing a novel without the letter "e" — *La Disparition,* or in the equally amazing English translation, *A Void.* "E" is, in short, an important letter.

One can imagine that for Twombly there was something satisfying about writing "e"s on a painting canvas. He wouldn't just write them; he would scratch and scrawl. He would write his "e"s and other letters as a primal act and as a childlike act. The scratch of letter was a gesture of meaning that didn't need anything else. This was painting doing language and when painting does language you don't get a book — you get the essence of the act stripped bare. Sometimes Twombly would just loop a drawn line around and around as if he was writing something but no distinct letters or words ever emerged. A number of Twombly's "gray paintings" from the late '60s and early '70s were like this. It is said that he would produce them by sitting on the shoulders of a friend and loop lines with his chalk while the friend wandered around in front of the canvas. What wonderful days those must have been. The loops must have felt big and airy, free and significant at the same time, the friend wandering around beneath, the light coming in through the window on a summer afternoon.

It is no surprise that the most important piece of writing on Cy Twombly is by the French theorist and occasional practitioner of semiotics, Roland Barthes. Semiotics, as the word suggests, is the study of signs. When Barthes was doing semiotics, he was decoding the signs of daily life, showing us what things really mean. But when Barthes came to the work of Cy Twombly, the crafty cryptologist, he realized that this would be no simple task of semiotics. Barthes realized that Twombly's paintings were acts of meaning without necessarily containing any specific meanings. Barthes wrote: "Words too belong to everybody; but sentences belong to writers: Twombly's 'sentences' are inimitable."

Twombly moved to Europe when he was 30 and lived in

different parts of Italy for most of his life. That makes sense. Language has a little bit more resonance in Italy because the history goes back so much further. A kid from Virginia would have noticed that. Twombly wanted to be able to throw out a word, or an image, and for that word or image to ripple out in waves of meaning with no clear direction or settling point, but with immense resonance. When you stand at a square somewhere in Rome and simply utter the name Virgil over and over again, you've already done a lot. Go to Rome, Twombly thought, and scrawl the name Virgil on a wall of an alley somewhere with a dirty pencil and you've done it all. What more could you want? You've just participated in things so big, so vastly meaningful in their resonance across human civilizations that you were lucky just to participate in that little piece of it. Just scrawling the name on a piece of paper is enough.

Roland Barthes noticed roughly the same thing about Twombly. "This is why Twombly's titles do not lead to analogy," Barthes wrote. "If a canvas is called The Italians, do not seek the Italians anywhere, except, precisely, in their name. Twombly knows that the Name has an absolute (and sufficient) power of evocation: to write The Italians is to see all the Italians."

He did see all the Italians, I think. Twombly painted canvases of such simple words and root images that the entire story of all human things is probably encoded in there. Maybe there are secrets about the future to be discovered in his canvases as well. I wouldn't put anything past the old cryptologist. We'll be looking at his scratches, scrawls, and beautiful marks for a long time to come.

By Morgan Meis
8 July 2011

David Weiss

(1946 – 2012)

Professor Butts walks in his sleep, strolls through a cactus field in his bare feet, and screams out an idea for a self-operating napkin.

The "Self-Operating Napkin" is activated when soup spoon (A) is raised to mouth, pulling string (B) and thereby jerking ladle (C), which throws cracker (D) past parrot (E). Parrot jumps after cracker and perch (F) tilts, upsetting seeds (G) into pail (H). Extra weight in pail pulls cord (I), which opens and lights automatic cigar lighter (J), setting off skyrocket (K) which causes sickle (L) to cut string (M) and allow pendulum with attached napkin to swing back and forth, thereby wiping chin."

— From a cartoon by Rube Goldberg

In a 1970 interview with Radio Smithsonian, the inventor, cartoonist, adjective, noun and pronoun Rube Goldberg told the story of how he began drawing the comic contraptions that now bear his name. He had told the story many times before. Goldberg was an engineering student and was taking a course in analytic mechanics. Goldberg's professor had asked his students to calculate the weight of the Earth. In the room was a humungous machine that the students were to use for this task. The whole room, Goldberg told the interviewer, was filled with retorts and Bunson burners and beakers and motors. And it suddenly occurred to Rube Goldberg: What could be more ridiculous than trying to figure out how much the Earth weighed? "I thought this was very useless," he would later say. But Goldberg thought it was funny, too. "That's the way people go," said Goldberg. "They go to a great extreme to accomplish very little."

Thereafter, Rube Goldberg began to have ideas for crazy useless machines and he started to draw them in cartoons. According to the dictionary, something is a "Rube Goldberg" if it "accomplishes by complex means what seemingly could be done simply." Goldberg's contraptions were pure satire, surprising combinations of people and things set up in a chain reaction that usually ended in the achievement of some mundane goal, such as the wiping of the chin. Goldberg didn't design his shaggy-dog machines to be built. They were meant to be mental mediations on the absurd. Such as the following:

At 6:30 weight (A) automatically drops on head of dwarf (B), causing him to yell and drop cigar (C), which sets fire to paper (D). Heat from fire angers dwarf's wife (E). She sharpens potato knife (F) on grindstone (G) which turns wheel (H) causing olive spoon (I) to dip repeatedly into olives. If spoon does not lift an olive in 15 minutes, clock (J) automatically pushes glass-cutter (K) against bottle and takes out a chunk of glass big enough for you to stick your finger in and pull out an olive.

Other Rube Goldberg machines reminded you to mail your wife's letter or turned off the lights for you or lit your cigar. Rube Goldbergs were mechanical slapstick. They lampooned the promise of technology, and the idea that technology is progress. The causes and effects in a Rube Goldberg are literally progressive, one thing happening upon another thing and another, like collapsing dominoes. At the same time, the contraptions expose human folly, the ways in which we're persistently falling over ourselves in a forward motion toward a predictably absurd finish. We act and act, and to what end? Let's remember, said a Rube Goldberg, there are more effective ways to clean one's chin and turn off the lights. Rube Goldberg surely would have found comedy in today's home computers, these highly sophisticated machines that are mostly used to say "Hello." The comedy of the Rube Goldberg is in the mundane ending. The elaborate game of physics that moves from ladle to cracker to skyrocket to sickle to pendulum just wouldn't be funny if it resulted in an extraordinary finish.

The fact that, almost a hundred years after Goldberg first began drawing them, people across the globe construct functioning Rube Goldbergs might be the funniest punch line of all. Rube Goldbergs now play a prevalent role in our pop culture (the 2010 OK Go video for "This Too Shall Pass" is a particularly magnificent example). But over the decades, Rube Goldbergs have changed in one important aspect: the endings have gone. The absurd teleology has disappeared. Rube Goldbergs are no longer technological satire; they are often just imaginative series of cascading events. Over the decades, as the machines transformed from ideas into actions, Rube Goldberg enthusiasts became less interested in spoof and more enchanted with the simple story of motion.

Recently, the co-creator of what is perhaps the most glorious Rube Goldberg of all, died. His name was David Weiss, half of the duo Fischli/Weiss. Fischli/Weiss' Rube Goldberg has been immortalized in 1987's art film *The Way Things Go* (Der Lauf der Dinge). In a Rube Golbergian way, it could be described like this:

In a warehouse in Switzerland two artists set up a slowly spinning bag of trash that (A) spins over a tire and pushes it, causing it to (B) roll into a weight attached to a board (C) which seesaws backward and pushes the tire further forward into another weight (D) which pushes a ladder forward into a bottle on the edge of a table (E) forcing it to tip over and send the table forward which (F) pushes it along a dolly that (G) bumps over an inflatable raft that...

And it goes on, in a 30-minute sequence. The components of *The*

Way Things Go are not funny; there are no dwarves or parrots or skyrockets. There are only everyday objects, choreographed to bump into each other, knock each other over, or light each other on fire. The film might be called "Stuff Falls Over, Stuff Burns." Yet, you can't imagine a more gripping 30 minutes. A balloon slowly deflates to release a cardboard tape roll that falls and initiates a slow chemical reaction that eventually lights a fire that lights a spark. A water balloon is slowly forced through a funnel and waddles to the ground, spilling a tray of foam. It is simple and spectacular. Usually, you don't know what's going to happen next, but more important, you don't know where it is all going. Even when the artists do show you the broom attached to the chair, you're never sure what the broom will do until it does. Often, an object appears to hesitate, as if questioning itself before finally letting go. Watching *The Way Things Go*, you laugh and hold your breath and cheer. The way the chemical reactions and newspaper fires help move tires along the floor is triumphant. In *The Way Things Go* gravity and motion are thrilling. Something happens, and then something else happens... Hooray! *The Way Things Go* is a story of heroism told without heroes. It is an adventure told through junk. Indeed, *The Way Things Go* tells such a strangely compelling narrative that many have insisted it must be a metaphor for something else: The French Revolution, a German professor once posed to the artists. Reincarnation and the transmigration of souls, a student in China suggested. But no, it is just the way things go.

The Way Things Go shows the extraordinariness of the ordinary. But it also emphasizes the way *we make* things go, for better or worse, whether we are creating a work of art or falling down a flight of stairs and landing on a cat or even standing still ("The Artist as Prime Mover" is what Arthur C. Danto called his essay on Fischli/Weiss). The forward motion of life, life as a chain reaction of cause-and-effect, is predictable; it is a cliché. Whatever we do or don't do, there will be cause and there will be effect. But as David Weiss once said in an interview, "There is something right about clichés." There is truth in the predictable. We can predictably learn to make things happen in a way that is predictably successful. Through repetition and work we can finally get the paint can to knock over the ladder. And yet, how that happens, the way it happens, is somewhat more mysterious.

"I've always found that astonishing..." David Weiss told *Frieze* magazine in 2006, "the way people always laugh when the next thing falls over."

"Strangely, for us," said partner Peter Fischli, "while we were making the piece, it was funnier when it failed, when it didn't work. When it worked, that was more about satisfaction."

The Way Things Go does tell a story about the satisfaction of success. Yet this story of success only happens through repeated failure. The trials and errors Fischli/Weiss went through to achieve 30 minutes of uninterrupted achievement are obvious. It is, of course, the possibility of failure that makes watching the falling objects so exciting. Just when you think that second tire can't possibly be moved by the second bag of trash, even though you've seen it work before, it does. As soon as the goal is achieved, we are ready for the next thing. The success, therefore, is satisfying, but the satisfaction is temporary.

Like many present-day Rube Goldbergs, *The Way Things Go* doesn't have a real ending, mundane or otherwise. A pail effectively tips into a bowl of what looks like dry ice. The mist froths over the sides of the bowl onto the floor, the camera pans away and there is a slow fadeout to credits. As the credits play, the sound of things going continues. Has it ended? Yes. Will it go on? Of course.

In contrast to Rube Goldberg's drawings, the punch line doesn't come at the end anymore. Instead, it's as if the entire process in *The Way Things Go* is one extended punch line. The punch line to the original Rube Goldberg cartoons carried a message: we ought to find simpler means to achieve our goals. Modern society has given us many convoluted ways to get what we want but, in the end, we'll live and die just like we always did. Those who have constructed real-world Rube Goldbergs, like Fischli/Weiss, take almost the opposite lesson: Be elaborate, be bold, be crazy, whatever the ending may be. The end is just a sideshow to the maddening, wonderful process of making things go. When engineers, artists, and regular people took the Rube Goldberg into their own hands and de-emphasized the punch line, the contraptions transformed from satirical gags into wonderful deeds.

It's possible Rube Goldberg quite understood the affirmative flipside embedded within his contraptions, knew that the people who merely laughed at the easy punch line were missing the point. A bit of Rube Goldberg trivia is that he wrote the first *Three Stooges* movie. The film had the excellent title *Rube Goldberg's Soup to Nuts*. The phrase "soup to nuts" is a culinary metaphor meaning from beginning to end. We start a meal with the soup and end with the nuts. But there's a metaphysics in the phrase, too. We start as soup and we will end as nuts. What do we do in the meantime?

"They have a big to-do when you're born," Rube Goldberg told Radio Smithsonian:

Father passes out cigars, and that is a big event. And there's also a big event when you die. Friends, everybody goes, goes to the funeral; they stand around and about you. But those two events are not as important as the thing in between.

[interviewer laughs]

The thing in between there is called life, and if you, if you use that, if you use that constructively and for all that it's worth, then, then I think you've got a good life. I don't think anybody's continually happy, uh, except idiots, you know.

By Stefany Anne Golberg
8 June 2012

Robert Hughes

(1938 – 2012)

Robert Hughes was macho. It is hard to point to any one thing that proves this assertion. He was just macho. He knew how to project authority and swagger. He would say tough-guy things like, "What strip mining is to nature the art market has become to culture." That is the primary reason he was always being compared to Clement Greenberg. Greenberg had that macho swagger too. Maybe it was the macho that allowed both Greenberg and Hughes to make such bold judgments about art, to proclaim what is good and what is bad. The macho was the antidote to the fear. It is inherently scary to be exposed to your fellow human being and Hughes, like Greenberg before him, exposed himself again and again. Before his death last week, Hughes had been the art critic for *Time* magazine for three decades. He is one of the few individuals of this era whose opinions on art were actually being read and considered by millions of people. The macho was a tool, a weapon in his arsenal. In this, he had learned a lot from reading Clement Greenberg.

For all the stylistic similarities between Hughes and Greenberg, Hughes was never (unlike, say, Michael Fried) a true Greenbergian. In an essay for *The New York Review of Books* in 1993, Hughes argued that, "There is little doubt that Greenberg's version of modernism has had its day. Not only because of the victories of what he dismissed as 'novelty art' — Pop, Minimalism, and media-based imagery of all kinds; but, more importantly, because of the limitations of his positivist world view, based on a truculent materialism." Hughes' critique of Greenberg was neither unique nor novel. Many artists and critics have come to realize that Greenberg's "formalism" was defined too narrowly, thus allowing contemporary art very little room to grow. But Hughes' essay from

1993 is notable in how directly he ties this critique of Greenberg into an analysis of Greenberg's youthful Marxism and its latent influence on his underlying conception of history. Hughes put it like this: "The experience of Marxism gave Greenberg his bent as a critic: an obsession with the direction of history."

And Greenberg was obsessed. It was impossible, for Greenberg, that art could be many things at once, that it could be exploring multiple dimensions. No. For Greenberg, History itself was moving art in one direction. The fact that painters after Manet were exploring the material nature of the paint and the canvas meant that this is what painting had become "about." This is what painting had to be. History itself had thrown content out the window. Any painter still painting "figures" and "scenes," still caught up in representational work, had failed to receive the message. History would leave them behind.

Hughes realized that, for all Greenberg's brilliance there was madness in this conception of art. At the same time, Hughes admired Greenberg's courage, his willingness to cut through the garbage and make a claim for what is serious and what is not. How, then, to discard the madness of Greenberg while retaining his courage and his commitment to sussing out what is honest and true in art?

Hughes took a bold and unusual approach. It is an approach not usually taken by the art critics of the Academy. It is an approach not often enough talked about in discussions of Hughes and his work. Hughes proposed, gently and with just so many qualifications, that any art that had lost all contact with nature was also in danger of losing its soul. He proposed, more daringly still, that "art may give access to a spiritual realm."

What did Hughes mean by "the spiritual realm?" I'm not sure Hughes himself was so clear about that. But he knew that the connection to nature and spirit was what could bring contemporary art back to life again. He knew it was the road out of empty formalism on the one hand and cynical postmodern game-playing on the other. Maybe Hughes' essay on the art of Frank Auerbach (also in *The New York Review of Books*, 1990) best captures Hughes sense of the spiritual route back out from the Greenbergian madness. Auerbach, Hughes thought, was of the belief that:

> Photograph by painting must "awaken a sense of physicality," transcend its inherent flatness, or fail. This was the opposite of the scheme of academic American criticism in the Sixties and Seventies, whereby modernism was supposed to move in a continuous ecstasy of self-criticism, under the sign of a purified, nondepictive flatness, toward the point where everything not "essential" to it had been purged. Auerbach believed in no such idea of art history, past, present, or to come.

The viewpoint that Hughes takes Auerbach to be attacking here is, of course, that of Clement Greenberg. Auerbach (for Hughes) was solving Greenberg's History problem by painting his way out of it, painting his way back to the world and away from the inherent flatness that Greenberg so adored. As Hughes writes about Auerbach in his lovely essay, his own language, just like Auerbach's painting, becomes richer and richer, more physical and descriptive over time. In one passage late in the essay, Hughes describes Auerbach's studio and the effect it has as a physical space.

> Images are pinned on the window wall and above the sink: a photo of Rembrandt's patriarchal head of an old bearded Jew, Jakob Trip, and another of Saskia; a small self-portrait by Auerbach's early friend and dealer Helen Lessore; a reproduction of Lucian Freud's head of Auerbach himself, the forehead bulging from the surface with tremendous, knotted plasticity; a drawing by Dürer of Conrat Verkell's head seen from below, the features gnarled and squeezed like the flesh structure in one of Auerbach's portraits; souvenirs of the work

of friends (Bacon, Kossoff, Kitaj) and of dead masters. They are all emblems and have been there for years, browned and cockled, like votives of legs and livers hanging in a Greek shrine.

Greenberg never wrote this way about art. He wouldn't allow himself to do it. Greenberg would have considered this kind of writing a disservice to the flat materiality of the tools and substance of art. But Hughes is in love with the physicality of his descriptions, with the historical and contextual relevance of creative spaces like Auerbach's studio. Here, art and life are interpenetrating all over the place. Hughes ends his essay on Auerbach by talking about Auerbach's tortured childhood and the loss of his parents to the Holocaust. We have come, by the end of the essay, to know something about Frank Auerbach the man and something about what made his life meaningful, what contact he had with pain and with suffering and with joy. "The deep family intimacy denied to him in boyhood," Hughes writes about Auerbach, "is summoned and reenacted in his work, in his hourly transactions with the object of scrutiny. 'To paint the same head over and over,' he will say, 'leads you to its unfamiliarity; eventually you get near the raw truth about it, *just as people only blurt out the raw truth in the middle of a family quarrel.'*" The italics are Hughes'. This may be a good a definition of the "spiritual realm" that Hughes felt art was capable of coming into contact with. It is the place where you get nearer the raw truth, a raw truth that is like what gets blurted out at a family quarrel.

Robert Hughes is dead now. His project, though, will live on. Hughes tried to drag art, kicking and screaming all the way, back toward the realm of deep meaning, back, you might say, to where it belongs.

By Morgan Meis
17 August 2012

Arthur Danto

(1924 – 2013)

Arthur Danto, the art critic for *The Nation* who died last month in New York, was a man with a big idea. Art, he believed, had ended. Of course, it is one thing to proclaim the end of art; it is another thing to prove it. But Danto tried. He was Johnsonian Professor of Philosophy at Columbia University, studied with Merleau-Ponty in Paris as a young man, and wrote a couple of books about analytical philosophy in his early career. Unusually for a postwar American philosopher, Danto thought a lot about Hegel. It was from Hegel that he got the idea that art could end. The idea that art has ended never meant, for Danto, that art has died or that people will not make art anymore. Just like Hegel did not mean by the "end of history" that the world was going to explode. "End" here means something more like "completion." The end of art means that the practice of making art has come to a historical culmination. The end of art means that art doesn't have a story, a narrative, anymore. After the end of art, there is no such thing as "Art" — there is only art.

Danto came to his realization about the end of art one day in New York City in the mid-1960s. Danto was himself painting in those days. He was also, as he readily admitted later, something of a snob and aesthete. One evening in the late spring of 1964, he stumbled into the Stable Gallery on 74th Street. At the Stable Gallery, Danto came face to face with Andy Warhol's *Brillo Boxes*. That's the sculpture where Warhol took some paint and some cheap wood and made a few *Brillo Boxes* that look exactly like Brillo boxes. That's to say, if you saw Warhol's *Brillo Boxes* on the ground outside of a deli in midtown you would simply think that a delivery person was moving Brillo boxes into the store. There is nothing in the *Brillo Boxes* to suggest anything but Brillo boxes.

Danto was struck and confused by *Brillo Boxes*. Over time, he worked out a full-blown theory to deal with them. The theory boils down to this: There is no way, visually, to know that *Brillo Boxes* is a work of art. So, the *Brillo Boxes* mark the moment when art became philosophy. You cannot look at the *Brillo Boxes* without asking the question, "What makes this art?"

When art became philosophical in the late spring of 1964, it crossed an invisible line. With the *Brillo Boxes*, there is no clear demarcation between art and reality. If *Brillo Boxes* can look just like Brillo boxes, and can still be art, then anything can be art. There is nothing inherent, nothing internal or necessary that makes something a work of art. Danto found this thought depressing at first. Art isn't special anymore if it can be anything.

Later, Danto came to see the end of art as a great liberation. He began to think of that day in 1964 as the day "when perfect artistic freedom had become real." The fact that art had ended meant that any artist could be:

an abstractionist, a realist, an allegorist, a metaphysical painter, a surrealist, a landscapist, or a painter of still lifes or nudes. You could be a decorative artist, a literary artist, an anecdotalist, a religious painter, a pornographer. Everything was permitted, since nothing any longer was historically mandated.

Danto took to calling this new and permanent era after the end of art the "Post-Historical Period of Art." It made him very happy.

I'm not sure the artists of the Post-Historical Period of Art are as happy about the end of art as Arthur Danto. Most of the artists I've known feel great anxiety facing the decision to make art with the knowledge that they can do and be anything. This kind of freedom can be immobilizing. I'm not sure that many artists fully grasp the link between the Hegelian moment when art became philosophical and the wide-open moment when art can be anything. Can't we simply say that art became fragmented and diverse just as many other things became fragmented and diverse in the course of Modernity? Do we need to identify some Hegelian culmination of history in a moment of philosophical self-understanding in order to account for the fact that there are no firm boundaries between art and non-art anymore? Probably we don't.

But Arthur Danto was writing and thinking himself out of a problem. He was having trouble accepting the art world as he found it. It might be said that he was having trouble accepting the world as he found it. *Brillo Boxes* were Danto's conversion moment. Danto wanted to be changed, to be transformed into a man who could see and understand the modern world around him. Danto's eyes were open, but he felt he could not see. He needed to convert himself in order to live.

There is a phrase that appears and reappears in the essays of Arthur Danto. That phrase is "the miraculousness of the commonplace." Danto wanted to feel that miracle. But he realized that he wasn't going to feel it by pretending that we are still surrounded by objects of high-aesthetic beauty. The modern world doesn't make great cathedrals, stone temples, or paintings to be worshipped in chapels and shrines. The modern world makes cheap shit out of plastic. But this was not the end of the story. Warhol's paintings of Coca-Cola bottles convinced Danto that the world of plastic and junk could be redeemed. Danto used this kind of language without apology. He said that Pop Art redeemed the world. He called Warhol's Campbell's soup cans "sacraments." Danto had been converted. He had good news to tell the rest of us.

I have the most vivid recollection of standing at an intersection in some American city, waiting to be picked up. There were used-car lots on two corners, with swags of plastic pennants fluttering in the breeze and brash signs proclaiming unbeatable deals, crazy prices, insane bargains. There was a huge self-service gas station on a third corner, and a super-market on the fourth, with signs in the window announcing sales of Del Monte, Cheerios, Land O Lakes butter, Long Island ducklings, Velveeta, Sealtest, Chicken of the Sea ... Heavy trucks roared past, with logos on their sides. Lights were flashing. The sound of raucous music flashed out of the windows of automobiles. I was educated to hate all this. I would have found it intolerably crass and tacky when I was growing up an aesthete. As late as my own times, beauty was, in the words of George Santayana, "a living presence, or an aching absence, day and night." I think it still is that for someone like Clement Greenberg or Hilton Kramer. But I thought, Good heavens. This is just remarkable!

How many times have any of us had the peace and acceptance to be able to look around us, confront the crap of daily life and say, "Good heavens. This is just remarkable!"? Before you raise your valid objections, let Danto have his moment. He achieved something there, as a man, as a human being on Earth trying to live in a world not chosen by him, but given. Thrown into a world of Velveeta and Chicken of the Sea, Danto found joy. Did he find too much joy? Did he surrender his critical edge in order to be amazed by Velveeta and Cheerios? That will always be the question with Danto.

But it is hard to fault him, since Danto's conversion made him into such a profoundly generous man. He had no bone to pick with art or artists anymore, not after he was redeemed by Pop. Writing art criticism for *The Nation*, Danto developed an almost uncanny ability to look at works of art on their own terms. He was sensitive to what the art was telling him, to what each work wanted to be. He was in dialogue with every work of art he ever saw. That's not to say he liked it all. But he always tried to let the work speak.

You might think, for example, that Danto would have had trouble with the art of Jenny Holzer. Holzer is best known for her electronic displays of short, often amusing and ironic sentences. A typical Holzer sentence is, "Abuse of Power Comes as No Surprise." It would be fair to say that much of Holzer's art is openly critical of the consumer society that Danto was trying to make his peace with. Here, however, is what Danto had to say about two Holzer exhibits in 1990:

> I find both exhibitions extraordinary and extraordinarily powerful, and though I am uncertain whether the bitter voices at the DIA or the platitudes at the Guggenheim have made me a better person, they have transformed me into an unqualified enthusiast for this odd artist.

I love the fact that Danto takes his shots here. He is "uncertain" whether he has been made a better person. In some ways, he doesn't like Holzer. We wouldn't expect him to. But he goes further. He forces himself into the work. He allows himself to be transformed. He wants to be transformed. By the end of the essay, Danto has said some incredibly penetrating and sensitive things about Holzer's work. He notices that Holzer resembles William Blake in taking language to be a physical thing, language as something you can see, and sometimes touch. The fact that Holzer put words onto surfaces makes her, in Danto's eyes, a special kind of visual artist. Danto sees Holzer as an artist who "exploits the tensions and sympathies between word and nonverbal medium." In the end, Danto realizes that Holzer's work operates on two different levels of aesthetic illusion. "Art," Danto says,

> was thought to be an illusion—fooling the senses ... Here, just because speech is the medium of truth, there is another order

of illusion: we falsely believe the words are addressed to us, and that, as with most words, they are asserted by the speaker and believed by her to be true. The work is consistently deeper than the words.

The collected essays of Arthur Danto are a sustained exercise in the kind of critical generosity he extended to Jenny Holzer. He always saw something fresh, startling, transformative. Every time. In talking about art, Danto was able to teach, a little bit, about how to live. I don't think anyone writing about art today can ignore what Danto achieved. He taught us how to be intelligent participants in the world as we find it. For those of us who still want to resist aspects of the world as we find it (politically, aesthetically, ethically), it has got to be done in Danto's spirit, with the tools he left behind. Is that a way of saying you have to learn to love the world, even if, especially if, you want to change it?

I will say one last thing. In my personal encounters with Arthur Danto, the redemption was for real. He had found something beautiful. You could see the twinkle sometimes in Danto's eyes. He was having fun loving the world. He was a man of grace. Strange grace manufactured through an unholy concoction of Hegel and Andy Warhol. But grace nonetheless.

By Morgan Meis
11 November 2013

James van Sweden

(1935 – 2013)

The 1940s suburban Michigan of James van Sweden's youth was a panorama of precise, tidy houses bordered by meticulous lawns. As a teenager, van Sweden was responsible for maintaining his parents' prized yard. The chore grew into a lawn-mowing business, which didn't last long. As van Sweden pushed his mower across his neighborhood, something else caught his attention. A few of his neighbors had allowed their yards to sprout free; the results were a revelation. Margaret Smith's lawn was "postage-stamp size," overtaken by larkspur and iris and globe thistle. Marybell Pratt and Margaret Holmes had almost no lawns at all. For James van Sweden, these neighbors were part of a tiny revolution. They secretly gave plants to the young van Sweden, who proceeded to overhaul the pristine backyard of his parents. Gone went the lawn and in its place waved tangles of wild phlox. Van Sweden began taking trips to the Michigan countryside, where he sketched country meadows and wildflowers, sand dunes and pines, re-imagining what a garden could be.

Like his Michigan neighbors, James van Sweden had a passion for grass. But van Sweden, with his landscape partner Wolfgang Oehme, wanted grass free-flowing and long, filled with birds and bees and butterflies. In his book *Gardening with Nature*, van Sweden included two paintings. One is *A Neat Lawn* by David Hockney. The centerpiece of *A Neat Lawn* is a house that is essentially a beige rectangle with an address on it. The house is flanked by static shrubs. The bottom half of the painting is another rectangle, a large green swathe of lawn. The grass is static and strangely barren. There are no people in *A Neat Lawn*, no movement at all, save a sprinkler lightly sprinkling.

The other painting in *Gardening with Nature*, by Edward Hopper, is titled *Cape Cod Evening*. It is also a painting with a house, but only the side of the house is seen. A man and a woman are relaxing in the evening light. The woman leans against the house with crossed arms; the man sits slouched on a step. A soft, overgrown grass yellowing with autumn hides their feet. They have obviously stopped mowing their lawn. There is a dog in the painting too, standing half-swallowed in the meadow that reaches back into a copse of woods behind the house.

James van Sweden wanted his gardens to be a holistic experience, something to stand in the middle of, be enveloped by, existing somewhere between art and wilderness. Van Sweden wanted to design gardens that had the boldness of a wild landscape, lush and full and free, gardens that moved even when the wind wasn't blowing, with dramatic contrasts of texture and height and color. Van Sweden thought a garden ought to have a powerful smell and include plants that you could stroke, like the velvety *Stachys byzantine*, which feels like the ears of a lamb. Touch was even more important to van Sweden than color, for human beings, he thought, are tactile creatures. Time's effect on the garden was paramount and each plant was carefully chosen in its relationship to the seasons. Some people thought Oehme and van Sweden's gardens most beautiful in winter. "Time is the gardener's friend and foe," wrote van Sweden, "always working its relentless changes. Gardening teaches us patience... But gardens can also teach us to live more in the moment — to listen, to watch, to touch, and to dream as the garden works its peaceful magic." Van Sweden thought a garden could be experienced like a poem or a story. There was meaning in every lichen-covered stone, every changing leaf, and that meaning could emerge from the same mystery contained in wild nature. "Out of vast, unknowable nature comes the freedom to form new thoughts, or to notice some tiny wonder for the first time... It is not necessary that meaning be written in the garden, only that you discover personal meaning and be transformed." Even a tiny garden plot on a tenement balcony could achieve the romance of a meadow, if given the right attention. Sometimes Oehme and van Sweden's New American Garden style was also called New Romantic.

For van Sweden, the words "American" and Romantic" were perfectly interchangeable. "Americans crave frontiers," he wrote in *Gardening with Nature*.

We like wide-open spaces, broad horizons, and new challenges. As a nation, we are restless wanderers, always searching for what's over the next rise. We put down roots only to pull them up again when the spirit moves us.

Given our love of change, it's surprising that the American garden scene consists mostly of suburban yards marching across the countryside in uniform ranks: hedges pruned carefully into unnatural boxes and balls; "foundation" shrubs piled high against houses like green concrete; broad, empty lawns awaiting weekly crew cuts and frequent doses of weed killer and water; and prissy flower beds jammed to their borders with garish and predictable annuals. Do gardens have to be so tame, so harnessed, so uptight?

For many Americans, these are hard words. The American lawn is not a mere domestic pleasure; it is the emblem of the civilized American. The American lawn is an ordering of savage nature, a triumph over the forces of chaos. Americans may once have craved frontiers, but the terror that wolves and mosquitoes wreaked upon early colonizers changed their intrepid self-conception. Prairies turned to city blocks, cowboys became urban planners, and geometry overcame anarchy. We paved over the chaos, drove out the insects, and shined fluorescent lights in the darkness. We are not to be entirely blamed for doing this. It is difficult to sit comfortably in a tangled meadow. People have no fur to speak of, no scales, no feathers. Our foot soles are soft, our nails are short, the meadow air makes us sneeze. Few things can soothe our tender hides and tender souls more effectively than the wide-open, broad horizon of a freshly mowed lawn.

Oehme and van Sweden understood that gardens were a balance between green concrete and totally wild nature. They would often allow garden paths to crop up organically, letting people wander as they liked and setting the path from this. Oehme and van Sweden were also not very strict about "natives." They liked North American plants but they liked exotic plants too. Both gardeners felt the Japanese had a particular sensitivity to grass. Oehme and van Sweden were broadminded when it came to grass. They loved Himalayan purple-silver grass and European autumn-moor grass as much as (or even more than) American grass.

Yet, American James van Sweden was ever guided by the spirit of "American grass." American grass, for van Sweden, is Thoreau and Whitman and wild Prairie shag. It is amber waves hiding the burial mounds of the Sioux and Grizzly bears and jackrabbits. This kind of grass was destroyed by the American lawn. Lawns took on the burdens and comforts of all things domestic. The wildness of grass went away, and with it that fabled wildness once said to reside in every American: The belief that one could, at any moment, go from settled to savage, that one could, at any moment, just go.

Wild grass was already on the way out in Thoreau's time. One of his most famous essays, "Walking," is largely a complaint about his neighbors' yards.

> Hope and the future for me are not in lawns and cultivated fields, in towns and cities, but in the impervious and quaking swamps... The most tasteful front-yard fence was never an agreeable object of study to me; the most elaborate ornaments, acorn tops, or what not, soon wearied and disgusted me. Bring your sills up to the very edge of the

swamp, then (though it may not be the best place for a dry cellar), so that there be no access on that side to citizens. Front yards are not made to walk in, but, at most, through, and you could go in the back way.

James van Sweden would have agreed with Thoreau about the problem but disagreed with his solution. For Thoreau, the only cure for the sterility of civilization was unspoiled wilderness. "In Wildness is the preservation of the World," he famously wrote. James van Sweden was able to find wildness in an un-mowed field. This is what James van Sweden meant when he wrote, "It is not necessary that meaning be written in the garden, only that you discover personal meaning and be transformed." James van Sweden thought grass, symbol of American sterility, could just as well resurrect the tamed American spirit.

"A child said, What is the grass?" wrote Walt Whitman, "fetching it to me with full hands;"

> How could I answer the child?. . . .I do not know what it
> is any more than he.
> I guess it must be the flag of my disposition, out of hopeful
> green stuff woven.
> Or I guess it is the handkerchief of the Lord,
> A scented gift and remembrancer designedly dropped,
> Bearing the owner's name someway in the corners, that we
> may see and remark, and say Whose?
> Or I guess the grass is itself a child. . . .the produced babe
> of the vegetation.
> Or I guess it is a uniform hieroglyphic,
> And it means, Sprouting alike in broad zones and narrow
> zones,
> Growing among black folks as among white,
> Kanuck, Tuckahoe, Congressman, Cuff, I give them the
> same, I receive them the same.

And now it seems to me the beautiful uncut hair of graves.

* * *

The grass in *Cape Cod Evening* is only a few inches longer than the grass in *A Neat Lawn*. It is yellowing instead of green. Both paintings are residential scenes: a house, a town, a lawn. Both paintings show nature in the hands of men. Only, in *Cape Cod Evening*, the grip has softened. The man in *Cape Cod Evening* holds his hand out to the dog but the dog looks the other way. The animal is just close enough to the couple to look comforted and just far enough away to look free.

By Stefany Anne Golberg
24 October 2013

John Updike
(1932 – 2009)

Updike gave a lecture on American art last year at the National Endowment for the Humanities. It was called "The Clarity of Things: What is American about American Art." Updike discussed how American painting finally managed to become American. Most of the early American painters were tradesmen. They knew how to paint, but they didn't know how to be "painterly." As Updike put it, they were "liney" in the beginning.

> A line is a child's first instrument of depiction, the boundary where one thing ends and another begins. The primitive artist is more concerned with what things are than what they look like to the eye's camera. Lines serve the facts.

Liney is how you paint when you know how to render individual things but you don't have the skill to make the depth and perspective cohere into a scene, to blur some of the hard lines in order to create a work of art. Still, there was something about liney painting that was true to the American experience. Speaking about the liney paintings of mid-18th-century painter John Singleton Copley, Updike said, "In the art-sparse, mercantile world of the American colonies, Copley's lavish literalism must have seemed fair dealing, a heaping measure of value paid in shimmering textures and scrupulously fine detail." But as America developed, so did its painters. They wanted to be able to paint like the masters across the sea. As ever seems the case in America, they had mixed-up desires: They wanted to be just as good as the Europeans and yet uniquely American. So American painters had to learn the subtle lessons of the craft all over again. Aesthetic problems that, in Europe, had been tackled and resolved in the early Renaissance became contemporary. Eventually, the American painters found a way. During the 19th century, they started making paintings that could easily have been created by European masters but for the slightly rougher subject matter of an American wilderness largely untamed. In doing so, they gained in skill at the expense of their specific style. To become better painters, they had to stop being so American.

As Updike saw it, it wasn't until the era of Abstract Expressionism that Americans came to a real ownership of painting, to a way of painting that was distinctly American: "And, to leap ahead ... into Abstract Expressionism, which for the first time in art history saw the United States decidedly shake off the influence of Europe and lead the way."

With Abstract Expressionism, American painters had discovered a way to be "liney" and "painterly" at the same time, on their own terms. Abstract Expressionism was like a fusion of that American desire to be self-sufficient and simple, without becoming provincial. Speaking of Rothko's painting *Number 10*, Updike noted that, "It has the two-dimensionality of liney work, but the rectangles would not float and intrigue the eye if they were less painterly, with the thin wash of variation within the central yellow panel and a casual dribble leaking from it; if the edges of were less feathery in their brushing, they would not hover in their ghostly way."

Updike never made the comparison, but there is a similar story to be told about American fiction. It all started in bewilderment and fear. There was, for all practical purposes, no such thing as an American literature until the mid-19th century. Nobody knew how to write in America, nobody knew what an American novel would look like, how it would sound. Nathaniel Hawthorne worried about that problem all the time. Eventually he grasped toward a kind of American Gothic, a version of Romanticism that was colored by the deep pull of the wilderness and the stark morality of Puritanism. That's not unlike what happened to the 19th-century painters. Romanticism — for the landscape painters — seemed like a way forward, a way to contribute to the European project and to be American at the same time. But they never achieved the full fusion between liney and painterly that would have to wait until Abstract Expressionism. Poe, Melville, Whitman — they all toyed around with this formula in their own ways. They produced legendary fiction, but it was the fiction of extremes. It never really touched upon the day to day, the simple mundane truths of a life lived on American shores. It was Henry James who finally achieved an exploration, in novel form, of the fine details of everyday American life. As he put it, "Experience is never limited, and it is never complete; it is an immense sensibility, a kind of huge spider-web of the finest silken threads suspended in the chamber of consciousness, and catching every air-borne particle in its tissue." James was able to capture this experience in prose by turning firmly back to English roots. He lived up to the title "novelist" to an almost scary degree. He was the personification of fiction, of the novel. But he had to give something up. He had turned himself into an English novelist. There are themes that ring out with an American tone, but the methodology, the sensibility, is essentially English. He once said, "However British you may be, I am more British still."

The early 20th century, too, produced its great American writers. From Dreiser to Norman Mailer, important works kept coming. But these were extraordinary times of world war and the creeping possibility of revolution and/or economic collapse. Normal life was to be suspended in the light of world events that outshone them. The task of writing about Americans in their daily lives would have to wait. Finally, the wars ended, the tumult subsided. American literature was ready to get back to the challenge of capturing the essential Americanness of people in non-extraordinary times.

That's where Updike came in. That's where Rabbit entered the stage. Rabbit, the now-immortal American jackass. Having tasted the extraordinary once —as a local basketball star in his high school days — Rabbit settled into the normalcy of suburban postwar American life. Vaguely unsatisfied and human — all too human — Rabbit was a person we hadn't heard very much from in American prose, at least not in American prose that was so clearly in dialogue with the great ones, that could produce pure artfulness on every page. "What Updike is saying — or conclusively demonstrating — is something very simple: that the unexamined life is worth examining." That's what Martin Amis had to say about Updike. It sums up Updike's literary project nicely.

A lot has been said, from Martin Amis to the obituaries popping up in every periodical, about Updike and his ability to write the experiences of the American middle class. There's no question this was his greatest accomplishment. Rabbit is so utterly recognizable as "one of us" that the novels seem to roll along with the barest of effort. It is more difficult, however, to figure out how Updike was able to accomplish the very thing that so many other talented writers could never quite get right. I think it has to do with the same kind of synthesis between "liney" and "painterly" that Updike talked about in his lecture. There are sentences in all of Updike's novels that can sit comfortably alongside anything written by Thomas Mann, or Robert Musil, or Marcel Proust. This from *Rabbit Redux*:

In winter, Pine Street at this hour is dark, darkness presses down early from the mountain that hangs above the stagnant city of Brewer; but now in summer the granite curbs starred with mica and the row houses differentiated by speckled bastard sidings and the hopeful small porches with their jigsaw brackets and gray milk-bottle boxes and the sooty ginkgo trees and the baking curbside cars wince beneath a brilliance like a frozen explosion.

There's an in-your-face confidence to that prose, a genius that can tell us small porches are "hopeful" and that parked cars can "wince." In passages like that, Updike revels in his skill, practically rubs our noses in it. This is Updike being "painterly." But he could be "liney," too. Updike never worried whether sentences of lyric beauty could perfectly well contain mundane specificity without losing anything. Here's the third sentence from *Rabbit, Run*: "The scrape and snap of Keds on loose alley pebbles seems to catapult their voices high into the moist March air blue above the wires." Another writer would have said "shoes" or maybe "sneakers" instead of Keds. They would have been afraid of the "Keds," of the specificity of the brand. They would have been scared that talking about Keds would have let the air out of the beautiful soaring balloon of a sentence they had created. Not Updike. And he's writing this in the late '50s. There's no sneer on his face either, no condescension to the fact that it matters, it matters that these kids playing basketball in the alley are wearing Keds. The Keds bring a lineyness to the sentence, a specificity that is true to an American experience in which brands and mass culture are written into our DNA. And still, even in their Keds, the voices of these boys catapult into moist March air blue above the wires. Updike's novels are filled with this synthesis, this blend between a universal soaring language and the everydayness that snaps the mind back into immediacy. The ease with which he brought the singular and the universal together is what really made him great.

The one passage that struck me as forced in re-reading *Rabbit, Run* is from the early part of the book where Rabbit first starts to run. He is driving away, trying to flee his stale marriage, heading to West Virginia simply to be heading somewhere. Updike writes:

On the radio he hears "No Other Arms, No Other Lips," "Stagger Lee," a commercial for Rayco Clear Plastic Seat

Covers, "If I Didn't Care" by Connie Francis, a commercial for
Radio-Controlled Garage Door Operators, "I Ran All the Way
Home Just to Say I'm Sorry," "That Old Feeling" by Mel
Torme, a commercial for Big Screen Westinghouse TV Set
with One-Finger Automatic Tuning...

The passage continues in this vein for another page or so. It is
forced because it reads simply as a list of references that haven't
been worked into the experience that Updike is describing. It
reminded me of John Dos Passos' great novel trilogy *USA*. I've
always admired the way that Dos Passos organized the novels in
alternating sections. The bulk of the books is constituted by the
ongoing stories of several characters, sometimes interweaving,
and the things that are happening to them as they go through life
in the period between the wars. Dos Passos alternates these
stories with what he calls Newsreels, which are essentially
fragments of headlines and newspaper columns and bits of
gossip giving a fragmented sense of the era. Then there are the
Camera Eyes, first-person, impressionistic glimpses of
experience. Occasionally, Dos Passos would throw in a brief
quirky biography of a notable figure of the time. Reading the
above passage from *Rabbit, Run*, I felt like I was reading one of
Dos Passos' Newsreels. But it also made me realize how much
Dos Passos' *USA*, brilliant as it is, is a kind of failure. Dos Passos
never came up with a sufficient technique by which the bits of
actual experience, the real stuff of the time, the names, the
brands, the popular songs, etc., could live in the individual
stories he was trying to tell. Dos Passos puts those things into his
novel, but he has to keep them separate, he has to show that they
are ultimately epiphenomenal to the "real" story.

Amazingly and consistently, but for the one passage in which
he resorts to that long list of stuff on the radio, Updike resists the
impulse to divide levels of experience. There is a kind of deep
metaphysical democracy to Updike's prose. The details matter,

the specific show being watched on television, the kind of car being driven, because those details are wrapped up in the substance of the experience. Here's a passage from *Rabbit At Rest*:

> He likes to pour salt out of the shaker until he has a heap and then rub the French fries in it, one by one. The French fries and about a pound of salt are all the kid eats; Harry finishes his Big Mac for him, even though he doesn't much care for all the Technicolor glop McDonald's puts on everything — pure chemicals. Whatever happened to the old-fashioned plain hamburger? Gone wherever the Chiclet went.

You can't overestimate how difficult it is to write about McDonald's that well. You can only write like this if you really care about the experience, if you take it seriously. Updike took it seriously. By flattening his metaphysics, by letting everything be essential, Updike discovered a new richness. He made the "painterly" and the "liney" one. In a funny way, I think the old guard, from Hawthorne to James, would have been proud. He solved the problem of American literature in ways that would have surprised them, but he did it. John Updike was a great American novelist.

By Morgan Meis
2 February 2009

Chinua Achebe

(1930 – 2013)

By the time the Nigerian novelist Chinua Achebe died late last month he'd taken on an official title: "Father of Modern African Literature." Achebe received this title mostly because of his novel *Things Fall Apart*, published in 1958. *Things Fall Apart* is often called the archetype of the African novel. It's a story of the Igbo peoples of southeastern Nigeria and British colonials who arrived to the area in the late 19th century. The Igbo people were trying to preserve their way of life. The British were trying to replace the Igbo way of life with their own. And that's how things fall apart.

Being dubbed the Father of Modern African Literature has its consequences. One consequence is that people start listening to what you have to say. So, when Chinua Achebe gave a lecture in which he said that Joseph Conrad was a "bloody racist," the world took note. Well, the literary world did, anyway. Achebe's lecture was entitled "An Image of Africa: Racism in Conrad's Heart of Darkness." He delivered the lecture at the University of Massachusetts Amherst in 1975.

Achebe's charge against Conrad is a serious one. He considered Conrad's short novel to be an instance of the Western desire to set up Africa as "a place of negations at once remote and vaguely familiar, in comparison with which Europe's own state of spiritual grace will be manifest." Achebe thought that Conrad had two basic metaphors for Africa, which Conrad returns to over and over again. The first is silence. The second is frenzy. Achebe takes two quotes from *Heart of Darkness* to illustrate the point. The "stillness of an implacable force brooding over an inscrutable intention." And, "The steamer toiled along slowly on the edge of a black and incomprehensible frenzy."

After Achebe delivered his lecture, the literary world delivered its hysteria. Articles were published. Books were written. Conferences were organized. Conrad was defended. Conrad was further denounced. Conrad was declared essential. Conrad was declared unreadable. In the end, both sides largely agreed upon two conclusions. Conrad was discovered to have been more or less a racist in his personal views. *Heart of Darkness* was discovered to be a tremendous piece of writing. Those two facts may sit uncomfortably together. But no one has yet figured out how to resolve them.

In all the hoopla over Conrad's racism, a strange irony went unnoticed. Conrad wrote a racist book that denounces the values of the civilization that produced racism. Achebe, on the other hand, attacked a racist writer using the values of the civilization that had created racism and which Conrad had denounced. Or we could put the irony another way. No one was more pessimistic about European civilization than Joseph Conrad. The characters of Conrad's novels are all, in some way or other, extremely uncomfortable with The West. Many of the characters are looking for a way out. Achebe, by contrast, had no desire to attack Western civilization as such. He was simply angry about Western racism and the dismissal of Africa as a place with its own legitimate culture and civilization. Achebe wanted the African story to be recognized, to be accepted as part of the broader civilizational story that Africa and Europe (and everyone else) can share.

The debate about Achebe and Conrad is thus a much deeper thing than the question of one man's racism. The debate is about the nature of civilization. Achebe himself points to these deeper questions in his essay. Here's how Achebe expresses the crucial problem:

The eagle-eyed English critic F. R. Leavis drew attention long ago to Conrad's "adjectival insistence upon inexpressible and incomprehensible mystery." That insistence must not be dismissed lightly, as many Conrad critics have tended to do, as a mere stylistic flaw; for it raises serious questions of artistic good faith. When a writer while pretending to record scenes, incidents and their impact is in reality engaged in inducing hypnotic stupor in his readers through a bombardment of emotive words and other forms of trickery much more has to be at stake than stylistic felicity.

Perhaps you'll have noticed that Achebe slipped in a rather large claim here. Achebe suggested that Conrad's "insistence upon inexpressible and incomprehensible mystery" must either be a stylistic flaw or outright artistic bad faith. What never crossed Achebe's mind is that the "insistence upon inexpressible and incomprehensible mystery" is the very nature and purpose of Conrad's literary endeavor. Both F. R. Leavis and Achebe are correct. Conrad does insist upon an inexpressible and incomprehensible mystery. He insists upon it very much. Conrad wrote book after book persisting in that insistence. The man was literally obsessed with the inexpressible and incomprehensible mystery.

Moreover, Conrad was aware that he was obsessed. Conrad once wrote a short preface to his confusing and barely readable novel *Nostromo, A Tale of the Seaboard*. In the preface, Conrad describes a feeling that had caused him to write the book. He was reading the autobiography of a sailor when a few sentences from the book made him remember his own life as a wanderer of distant oceans. Conrad, after all, spent 20 years as a sailor for the French and English merchant navies before he ever began to write. Here's how Conrad describes the memories the sailor's autobiography evoked: "bits of strange coasts under the stars, shadows of hills in the sunshine, men's passion in the dusk, gossip half-forgotten, faces grown dim." These few words are basically a condensed version of every novel and short story Conrad ever wrote. By the standards of most novelists, it is hazy and insubstantial material. What exactly is Conrad trying to say? But then we come back to Achebe's quote from F. R. Leavis. Conrad isn't saying anything. He is insisting, insisting upon the inexpressible and incomprehensible mystery at the heart of experience.

The heart of the mystery of existence is the place of the greatest inexpressibility and the most maddening incomprehensibility. It is, for Conrad, where darkness threatens to take over completely. Conrad firmly believed that the more you peel away layers of civilization, the closer you come to the heart of the mystery. At the heart of the mystery is a truth, a truth of who we are, of the inner nature of human existence. But the darkness at the heart of that truth means that the closer you get the less you can see. The deepest truths are necessarily obscure. Conrad felt drawn to that mystery, to that truth, and to that darkness even as he was terrified and repelled. As a writer, he explored the push and pull of this compulsion over and over again.

In writing about inexpressible mysteries, Conrad entertained a fantasy of Africa, not hard to find among Westerners — either then or now — as a place outside of civilization. A primal place. Marlow's trip down the river in *Heart of Darkness* is a trip into prehistory. As Marlow and his steamboat full of white people move further down the Congo, they come into contact with the people of Africa.

> But suddenly as we struggled round a bend there would be a glimpse of rush walls, of peaked grass-roofs, a burst of yells, a whirl of black limbs, a mass of hands clapping, of feet stamping, of bodies swaying, of eyes rolling under the droop of heavy and motionless foliage. The steamer toiled along slowly on the edge of a black and incomprehensible frenzy. The prehistoric man was cursing us, praying to us, welcoming us — who could tell?

Achebe makes a biting and very funny comment about this passage. Achebe wonders whether there isn't "abundant testimony about Conrad's savages which we could gather if we were so inclined from other sources and which might lead us to think that these people must have had other occupations besides merging into the evil forest or materializing out of it simply to plague Marlow and his dispirited band." In fact, that is what Achebe does in *Things Fall Apart*. Achebe tells the actual living stories of people who exist in Conrad's book only as "a whirl of black limbs." It turns out the people of African villages had quite a lot to do other than "merging into the evil forest or materializing out of it." In that sense, Achebe's book is a lovely counter-story to Conrad's book. Every time an incomprehensible black man wanders off into the bush in Conrad, you can pick up his story in Achebe.

But therein lies the fundamental difference between the two writers. Achebe wants to tell comprehensible stories. Moreover, Achebe feels morally and politically compelled to tell a comprehensible story of African life. He does not want Africa to carry the burden of being the dark and incomprehensible continent. The opening sentence of Achebe's *Things Fall Apart* reads, "Okonkwo was well known throughout the nine villages and even beyond." The fact that Okonkwo was well known means, at the very least, that he is knowable. Achebe is going to make Okonkwo knowable to us. And he does. Okonkwo is a brother to us by the time we've finished reading *Things Fall Apart*.

But here's a passage again from *Heart of Darkness*. Marlow has paused in his narration and seems unable to go on. He says:

...No, it is impossible; it is impossible to convey the life-sensation of any given epoch of one's existence, — that which makes its truth, its meaning — its subtle and penetrating essence. It is impossible. We live, as we dream — alone.

Marlow is not well known throughout the nine villages, nor anywhere else. He is fundamentally incomprehensible, even to himself. At the end of *Heart of Darkness* Marlow attempts to tell the wife of the man he'd been looking for in the jungle (Kurtz) what happened to her husband. He cannot. The experiences of the woman in London and the man off in a remote part of the Congo are incommensurable. This is the one part of Conrad that Achebe simply got wrong. Conrad does not think that the experiences of London and Congo are incommensurable because one is good and one is bad. Conrad does not think that Africa is the negation of Europe's "spiritual grace" as Achebe puts it. To the contrary, Conrad thinks you have a better chance at catching a glimpse of the reality of existence on a river in Africa than you do on the river Thames. But the glimpse is only ever a glimpse nonetheless. In *Heart of Darkness*, Conrad gives a name to this glimpse of the reality of existence. They are probably the most famous words in the book. "The horror!" Kurtz says with his dying breath, "The horror!" It is important that the words are repeated. "The horror" said once is an expression of shock and dismay. "The horror" said twice is a pronouncement, an oracle, simultaneously elusive and definitive. What does it mean? It can't be put into other words. That's why Kurtz repeats it. It is a statement that has reached the very bedrock. Marlow's attempt to communicate any of this to the dead Kurtz's wife back in London is a complete failure. The wife is convinced that Kurtz was a great man. Marlow knows him to have been pitiful and cruel:

> The sound of her low voice seemed to have the accompaniment of all the other sounds, full of mystery, desolation, and sorrow, I had ever heard — the ripple of the river, the soughing of the trees swayed by the wind, the murmurs of wild crowds, the faint ring of incomprehensible words cried from afar, the whisper of a voice speaking from beyond the threshold of an eternal darkness.

Kurtz's wife asks Marlow what were Kurtz's last words. Marlow knows them to have been "The horror! The horror!" "The last word he pronounced was," Marlow hesitates, "your name." Marlow can't tell Kurtz's wife the truth, mostly because he doesn't know how to put that truth into language. And that is how Marlow ends his story, the story that is *Heart of Darkness*. Conrad writes, "Marlow ceased, and sat apart, indistinct and silent, in the pose of a meditating Buddha." Those are four favored words in the Conrad arsenal, "ceased," "apart," "indistinct," and "silent." Just more words that circle around an "inexpressible and incomprehensible mystery," and then, finally, fall silent altogether.

It has often been said that Chinua Achebe gave Africa a voice. It is not hard to see the truth of this statement in reading *Things Fall Apart*. Achebe's amazing accomplishment in that novel is to use a mostly European art form, the novel, to tell an African story. The story of Okonkwo is told on his terms. Achebe explains in sparse prose what Okonkwo did and how he felt. Rituals, traditions, and stories are described in a straightforward manner in the voice of someone who assumes they will make sense. For this reason, they do make sense. At the heart of Achebe's novel is the unexpressed belief in the clarity of stories. Okonkwo's story is terrible in the end, a story of collapse. But the collapse is all the more tragic given what we find out in the novel — that Okonkwo is knowable and that the story of his life is one we can share. The tragic story of *Things Fall Apart* is thus a story of light, it has a heart of lightness. We can see it.

It is not surprising that a man with a heart of lightness should feel poorly disposed toward a man with a heart of darkness. But it strikes me that the two writers created central characters who share something real. Both Marlow and Okonkwo finish their stories by falling into silence. Experience has been too much for them. In this, Marlow and Okonkwo have something to communicate to one another. But it is something the rest of us can only hear "as a faint ring of incomprehensible words cried from afar."

By Morgan Meis
15 April 2013

David Foster Wallace

(1962 – 2008)

Nobody ever really knows why someone else commits suicide — that's what makes it an ultimate act, an unsettling challenge to those of us who keep on. Anyway, it doesn't matter why. The death of David Foster Wallace is simply a fact now and we're the ones who have to deal with it.

I fear that we didn't do very well by David. We didn't listen to him closely enough and we kept making him into something that he wasn't. We called him an ironist. We suggested, often enough, that he was part of The Problem. Or we simply dismissed him as a cute and funny writer with a number of tricks up his sleeve. It was true, of course, that he never came up with a solution — no one has. But he dedicated himself to the problem of America, how to write about it, how to care about it, how to negotiate between loving it and hating it.

Because he was reasonably honest, he ended up taking crap from all sides. To the cultural conservatives he was everything bad about postmodernism. To the postmodernists, he was the wunderkind and court jester who served literary pleasure. But he was neither. He was never willing to fall into either of those camps.

David Foster Wallace has left us with quite a few great essays. Perhaps none is as great as the piece "E Unibus Pluram: Television and U.S. Fiction," collected in *A Supposedly Fun Thing I'll Never Do Again*. I think of it as an anti-manifesto. It is the painstaking elucidation of a genuine conundrum. I call it a genuine conundrum because there is a difference between simply being confused and having earned your confusion. In "E Unibus Pluram," Wallace lets himself think about literature as a task, literature as something each generation has to try and get right. Bravely, he begins the essay talking about television. He likes television. Goddamit we all like television. He will not join the ranks of those who simply dismiss the boob tube as nothing more than that. Or as Wallace puts it, laconically, "American literary fiction tends to be about U.S. culture and the people who inhabit it." For Wallace, the central problem is not whether television is good or bad. Television, he wants to say, is constitutive of who we are, and that which is constitutive of who we are is beyond simple value judgments — it has become the necessary ground from which we proceed. You can't be a writer, you can't write about how the people around you experience the world, without taking into account that simple but massively important fact. You have to deal with television and other aspects of American popular culture, truly deal with it. And yet, Wallace doesn't want to be reduced to television. He is confused about just how much he should accept it and how much he should reject it. He is trying to find the right balance in the midst of his confusion.

His writing sensibility is thus born from the "Metafiction" movement of the '60s. These were the guys who tried to confront a new America with a new literature. In short, these writers (Pynchon, Barth, etc.) were willing to put television and consumer culture into the heart of their literary endeavors. As he writes in "E Unibus Pluram":

> Metafictionists may have had aesthetic theories out the bazoo, but they were also sentient citizens of a community that was exchanging an old idea about itself as a nation of doers and be-ers for a new vision of the U.S.A. as an atomized mass of self-conscious watchers and appeasers. For metafiction, in its ascendant and most important phases, was really nothing more than a single-order expansion of its great theoretical nemesis, Realism: If Realism called it like it saw it, Metafiction simply called it as it saw itself seeing itself see it.

That's very funny, but funny-true. The main point is that we really don't have much of a choice. If you're going to confront the world and then write about it you're going to have to confront people as they are. In fin de siècle America, no one is spending time gazing at the countryside in a coach from Moscow to St. Petersburg.

Wallace was also willing to recognize that this puts literature in a tricky situation. A society of television watchers, and watchers watching ourselves watch, is always going to be in danger of producing a literature that is itself caught up in that dialectic. Wallace watched it happening. He watched his literary forefathers, writers like Pynchon and Gaddis, get caught up in the game of ironic distancing that itself had already been mastered by the cultural mainstream they were trying to critique. That was one side of Wallace's critique of irony. He was suspicious of an irony that pretends it has the answers and confronts the world in the basic mood of paranoia and mockery. There is no real outside, he realized. There is no place above it all from which literature can speak to the world.

> It won't do, then, for the literary establishment simply to complain that, for instance, young-written characters don't have very interesting dialogues with each other, that young writers' ears seem "tinny." Tinny they may be, but the truth is that … [w]hat most of the people I know do is they all sit and face the same direction and stare at the same thing and then structure commercial-length conversations around the sorts of questions that myopic car-crash witnesses might ask each other — "Did you just see what I saw?"

And allow me a brief aside here. In recognizing that American fiction really had to deal with the experiences of actual Americans, Wallace taps into an old theme of American literature. To wit, he's still wondering what it is about the American experience that makes it American (Is it special? Is it unique? Can it compete with the others?). There's a great short essay by Malcolm Cowley called "The Middle American Prose Style." In it, he traces an American literary voice from Hemingway back to Twain, and ultimately to the stories of David Crockett that were collected and published in the early 19th century. Cowley notes two things in particular. One, that from Crockett on there is a "habit of making flat assertions about their emotional reactions that come after a series of violent images and therefore give the effect of understatement." Well, this is the same thing that Wallace is talking about with the people sitting around together watching extraordinary things on television and then asking each other, relatively dispassionately, whether others saw it, too. Cowley's second main observation is that there is a certain attention to a spoken vernacular and its inherent repetition in the Crockettian prose style. Cowley says, "neither did Gertrude Stein invent the trick of repeating the same word in several sentences, so that it gives a keynote to the paragraph. Crockett found the trick instinctively..." Well, just look at a phrase from the above quote from Wallace: "What most of the people I know do is they all sit and face the same direction and stare at the same thing and then..."

Wallace's innovation is that he takes this "Middle American Prose Style" and he applies it to the contemporary situation in which "Middle American Experience" isn't quite so simple anymore. It has been wrapped over on itself a couple of times due to all the watching and the watching of the watching. It has also been complicated by history and by good times and bad times and back again a couple of cycles through. There's no frontier anymore, in the land or in the mind. The imagination runs up against itself. Wallace faced up to that state of affairs and pushed the "Middle American Prose Style" where it needed to go in response.

But writing purely from the inside was never satisfying to him either. That is the other side of Wallace's critique of irony. He never liked irony in its Kierkegaardian mode, in its refusal to take on any position in the glib knowingness that everything might as well be everything else. This is where he would get angry at the people who simply aped the language and the attitudes that they observed around them. He didn't want to drown in that mess.

And so, funnily enough, David Foster Wallace ended up searching for a new way to be a realist, just as so many generations of writers have done before him. He wanted to get hold of what it's like to be a person in this particular world without either dismissing the vast sea of commercial and popular culture we live in or pretending that we don't often feel uneasy swimming around in that sea. He wanted to take that sea seriously as the ground and condition of our experience without thereby being taken in by everything it says about itself. This left him with few genuine allies in the cultural battles of the last two decades. And I don't think he ever felt that he had worked his way out of that dilemma. It was operating on him, I suspect, until the day he died.

He once said in an interview, "I don't think I'm talking about conventionally political or social action-type solutions. That's not what fiction's about. Fiction's about what it is to be a fucking human being." I take this phrase "a fucking human being" to be something of a technical term in Wallace's thinking. A fucking human being is a human being who is right in the middle. A fucking human being grew up and learned basic attitudes and gestures of being human partly by watching television. And then things got more complicated. A fucking human being finds it easy to slip into the sensibility of any Joe Sixpack coming home from a day at work but simultaneously really wants to know exactly what it feels like and how it works itself out internally to be just such a person. A fucking human being is constantly struggling to find the proper approach by which one can accept the weirdness of contemporary life as real, while at the same time saying something real, something true, about it.

I'm sorry, David, that we didn't always care for you in the way that we should have. We assumed too often, and with a notable lack of empathy and perception, that you were having fun tossing yourself around on the waves of our contemporary discontent. But you meant it and you were always going for a literature that means it. You weren't like so many of the others. You were a fucking human being.

By Morgan Meis
19 September 2008

Tom Clancy

(1947 – 2013)

Tom Clancy's death did not shake the literary establishment. That's because Tom Clancy was never part of the literary establishment. He was an insurance salesman. In his spare time, Clancy wrote military thrillers. His first book, *The Hunt for Red October* — about a Soviet naval officer who takes his super-secret sub and defects to the US — was published by the Naval Institute Press in Annapolis. Clancy got 5000 bucks for it. But Ronald Reagan read the book and started telling everybody how much he loved it. Soon enough, Clancy was a bestselling author. The story gets ridiculous from there, with books spilling off the presses and hundreds of millions of dollars changing hands. Movies were made. Video games were made. This was the stuff that publishers and business-minded authors dream about on cold autumn nights.

The more famous Tom Clancy became, the more serious readers ignored him. Clancy was, after all, not so much a writer as a teller of war stories. He wrote to get the story down. Beyond that, he had little sense of craft or style. He wrote his stories. He made his money. And then he died. The end.

There is, however, a tantalizing side note to this story. There was a man whose death did very much shake the literary establishment. That man was David Foster Wallace. And David Foster Wallace, it turns out, liked to read Tom Clancy. That's no big deal, you might say. Even the most serious writer needs to take a break from reading Dostoyevsky and Wittgenstein, and we all enjoy a good potboiler. True enough. Except that DFW seems to have valued Tom Clancy a lot more highly than that.

There is, for instance, the now notorious top-ten list of favorite books that David Foster Wallace put together before his death in 2008. The list includes such books as *The Screwtape Letters* by C.S. Lewis, and *Fear of Flying* by Erica Jong. Not the books you might have guessed DFW would put on a top-ten list, but not completely surprising. Then, at number ten, sits a book by Tom Clancy: *The Sum of All Fears*. That's the book where Clancy's famous character, Jack Ryan of CIA, has to foil a terrorist plot to detonate a nuclear device on American soil. You may have seen the movie with Ben Affleck and Morgan Freeman.

DFW considered this book by Tom Clancy serious enough reading put it on a top-ten list of all-time favorites. We're challenged to figure out why. The writer D.T. Max recently wrote a biography of DFW called *Every Love Story Is a Ghost Story: A Life of David Foster Wallace*. Max has claimed (in a *New Yorker* article) that DFW "admired the novels of Tom Clancy for their ability to pack in facts." It is not, on the face of it, a very revealing comment. What exactly does it mean to "pack in facts," anyway?

But on second thought, it is revealing. DFW loved to pack in facts with his own writing. He had real trouble deciding just how many facts to include. Hundreds of pages were ultimately cut from his first novel *The Broom of the System*, and from his magnum opus *Infinite Jest*. It was a desire to include many facts that led to one of DFW's most loved (and most criticized) formal inventions, the footnote (or endnote). DFW could put a footnote in anything: a casual essay, a novel, a short story. DFW's footnotes and endnotes sometimes take up more space than the main body of the text. DFW published, for instance, a review of dictionaries and English-usage books for *Harper's Magazine* in 2001 (later included in his essay collection *Consider the Lobster*). The review includes 52 notes, some of which get into long discussions about grammar and syntax and are short treatises in themselves. Note 23 is an explanation of Wittgenstein's private language argument. It reads, in part:

The point here is that the idea of a Private Language, like

Private Colors and most of the other solipsistic conceits with which this particular reviewer has at various times been afflicted, is both deluded and demonstrably false.

In the case of Private Language, the delusion is usually based on the belief that a word such as pain has the meaning it does because it is somehow "connected" to a feeling in my knee. But as Mr. L. Wittgenstein's *Philosophical Investigations* proved in the 1950s, words actually have the meanings they do because of certain rules and verification tests that are imposed on us from outside our own subjectivities, viz., by the community in which we have to get along and communicate with other people.

That paragraph ends with the sentence, "Wittgenstein's argument, which is admittedly very complex and gnomic and opaque, basically centers on the fact that a word like 'pain' means what it does for me because of the way the community I'm part of has tacitly agreed to use 'pain'." That happens to be the best single-sentence explanation of Wittgenstein's private-language argument that I am aware of.

The point of all this is simple. DFW had many things to say. He wanted to say them all and he had trouble fitting in all the facts. This caused him to use sometimes tortuous and complicated grammatical structures and to look for various ways, like footnotes, to get all the information in. DFW looked to the writing of Tom Clancy and found a similar obsession with information. Clancy also had a lot of things to say. He loved technical manuals and he loved to find out how things work — guns and big machines like aircraft carriers, yes, but also people and organizations. Here, for example, is a passage from a climactic scene at the end of Clancy's *Clear and Present Danger*.

"Uh-oh," the flight engineer said. "I think we have a P3 leak here. Possible pressure bleed leak, maybe a bad valve, number-two engine. I'm losing some Nf speed and some Ng, sir. T5 is coming up a little." Ten feet over the engineer's head, a spring had broken, opening a valve wider than it was supposed to be. It released bleed air supposed to recirculate within the turboshaft engine. That reduced combustion in the engine, and was manifested in reduced Nf or free-power turbine speed, also in Ng power from the gas-producer turbine, and finally the loss of air volume resulted in increased tailpipe temperature, called T5.

Now, most thriller writers would have taken care of this passage with the phrase, "the plane was in trouble." But not Clancy. He loved all the details and he was damned if he was going to cut anything out. Clancy wrote like this all the time, in all of his books. Right in the middle of the action he would simply break off into laborious and overly technical explanations of the mechanical workings of a plane or the Byzantine hierarchical structure of the NSA.

I suspect that DFW was jealous of the way that Clancy simply stuffed it all in. No footnotes. No elaborate syntax. The incredible thing about reading Tom Clancy is that there is never a shift in register. One moment he is explaining what the characters are doing within the plot of his novel, the next moment he is taking several pages to describe how a fighter jet lands on an aircraft carrier at night. Then he jumps back to the plot again. The lack of transition, the non-sequiturs, never bothered Clancy. *Clear and Present Danger* comes in at 688 pages in my paperback copy. And that is with very small type. The story could have been told in 200 pages. That makes roughly 488 pages of information-packing.

So, when DFW said that he admired the novels of Tom Clancy for their ability to pack in facts, he was expressing a genuine admiration. This forces the rest of us to recognize that Clancy and DFW are of a similar type. They are fact lovers and information gatherers. And they were both faced with hard challenges as writers of fiction. DFW was a philosopher and a thinker. He solved his problems through formal innovations and tortuous bouts of self-reflection. Clancy was a highly intelligent man, but he was not of a philosophical bent, he was not given to bouts of self-reflection. He had more of an engineer's mentality, the desire to figure out how things work. But the love of facts made the two writers brothers. When you imagine either DFW or Tom Clancy in the process of writing, you have to imagine them with a child's eagerness, jumping up and down in the school chair and raising their hand to tell the teacher something she didn't know.

* * *

There have always been writers who love information. These writers do not know when to leave it alone, when to put the pen down. This is their glory and their pain. Pliny the Elder, the Roman writer and historian of the 1st century CE, was a man like DFW and Tom Clancy. Pliny's *Natural History* is a work that tries to say a little something about everything, from botany to the history of painting. Pliny will jump from one subject to the next, often in the middle of a thought. No matter. The next thought has become even more interesting to him than the last. There is a loose structure to *Natural History*, but the work mostly proceeds at the pace of Pliny's own mind. It is said that Pliny had a special chair made so that he could continue writing even as his servants took him out for daily walks. He had special gloves made to write on cold days. He wrote in the bath, on the toilet. He could not stop the flow of information.

Or think of Victor Hugo. *Les Misérables* contains close to 20 chapters on the Battle of Waterloo. Hugo goes into great detail explaining specific moments and turning points at Waterloo. He fights with other commentators and scholars about the meaning and significance of the battle. He writes a short book, in essence, about Waterloo and then sticks that book into the much longer book *Les Misérables*. And that is not the only digression in the book. The ratio between actual plot in *Les Misérables* and digressions is probably about the same as in *Clear and Present Danger*. The digressions win out by a long shot.

Or think of Honoré de Balzac and his *La Comédie humaine* (*The Human Comedy*). This is the series of novels written by Balzac with the goal of encompassing all of French life in the early to mid-19th century. In a letter to a friend, Balzac wrote of one of the books of *The Human Comedy* that it should "represent social effects, without a single situation of life, or a physiognomy, or a character of man or woman, or a manner of life, or a profession, or a social zone, or a district of France, or anything pertaining to childhood, old age, or maturity, politics, justice, or war, having been forgotten." After that, he planned to start writing a series of books on the history of the human heart and then a series on the causes of all things in life. Balzac died, in the summer of 1850, of exhaustion.

What is it that drives all of these writers? What pushes them into such a mania for information and detail that it threatens to overwhelm the very literature they are trying to write? Metaphysics lingers behind this obsession for information. The metaphysics is the underlying intuition that everything matters because everything is connected to everything else. You could call this holism. But it isn't a firm doctrine in the hands of such writers as DFW, Clancy, Hugo, and Balzac. They don't have a theory so much as a gut feeling. All is one. All is a necessary part of greater whole. Every detail is part of a story that ought to be told. Every fragment of existence is like a thread through which the entirety of the cosmos can be traced.

This means that there is really no such thing as a digression for these writers. Victor Hugo says it in the very first words of *Les Misérables*:

In 1815, M. Charles-Francois-Bienvenu Myriel was Bishop of

D — He was an old man of about seventy-five years of age; he had occupied the see of D — since 1806. Although this detail has no connection whatever with the real substance of what we are about to relate, it will not be superfluous, if merely for the sake of exactness in all points, to mention here the various rumors and remarks which had been in circulation about him from the very moment when he arrived in the diocese. True or false, that which is said of men often occupies as important a place in their lives, and above all in their destinies, as that which they do.

Do you see the obsession in these lines, the idea that everything matters and that everything is, in the end, relevant to everything else? The poetic version of this opening salvo by Hugo in *Les Misérables* can be found in Baudelaire's famous poem, "Correspondences":

Nature is a temple where living pillars
Let escape sometimes confused words;
Man traverses it through forests of symbols
That observe him with familiar glances.
Like long echoes that intermingle from afar
In a dark and profound unity,
Vast like the night and like the light,
The perfumes, the colors and the sounds respond.

Tom Clancy would never have worded it this way. DFW had his own, much more colloquial language. But it is the "dark and profound unity" that all the information lovers are after. When DFW read *The Sum of All Fears* he read the words of a kindred writer who could not stop pulling at the threads of information. Clancy had a deep faith that the sometimes disparate threads of information would make his writing richer, more real, more adequate to the deep and abiding mysteries of life. That is why writers like DFW and Clancy keep casting out into the abyss of too-much-information and then clawing their way back to the story they are supposed to be telling. All the threads are connected in a dark and profound unity. The only hope for a writer trying to touch upon that unity is to pack in as many facts as possible. The facts could never lead writers like DFW and Clancy astray for one simple reason: There is nowhere to stray to when all is one.

By Morgan Meis
15 October 2013

Susan Sontag

(1933 – 2004)

In an essay about the Polish writer Adam Zagajewski, Sontag writes that as Zagajewski matured he managed to find "the right openness, the right calmness, the right inwardness (he says he can only write when he feels happy, peaceful.) Exaltation—and who can gainsay this judgment from a member of the generation of '68—is viewed with a skeptical eye." She's writing about what Zagajewski was able to achieve but she is also, of course, writing about herself.

Sontag was also a member of the generation of '68, if a slightly older one. She too achieved an openness, calmness, and inwardness as she matured, though it came with regrets and the sense that the pleasure of a literary life is an ongoing battle against a world that is predisposed to betray that pleasure.

Writing about Zagajewski again, she explains that his temperament was forged in the fires of an age of heroism, an ethical rigor made sharp by the demands of history. These men and women spent decades trying to write themselves out of totalitarianism, or they were trying to salvage something of their selves from what Sontag does not hesitate to call a "flagrantly evil public world." And then suddenly, in 1989, it was all over. The balloon popped, the Wall came down. Wonderful events, no doubt, but with the end of that era came the end of the literary heroism made possible by its constraints. Sontag says, "how to negotiate a soft landing onto the new lowland of diminished moral expectations and shabby artistic standards is the problem of all the Central European writers whose tenacities were forged in the bad old days."

Sontag also managed to come in softly after scaling the heights of a more exuberant time. In her case, she wasn't returning to Earth after the struggle against a failing totalitarianism, she was coming down from the '60s. But that is one of the most remarkable things about her. Not everyone was able to achieve such a soft landing after the turbulence and utopian yearnings of those years.

Sontag's early writings are shot through with a sense of utopian exaltation, an exaltation so often associated with the '60s. In her most ostensibly political work, "Trip to Hanoi", she talks specifically about her mood in those days. As always, she is careful not to overstate things. "I came back from Hanoi considerably chastened," she says. But then she goes on, heating up. "To describe what is promising, it's perhaps imprudent to invoke the promiscuous ideal of revolution. Still, it would be a mistake to underestimate the amount of diffuse yearning for radical change pulsing through this society. Increasing numbers of people do realize that we must have a more generous, more humane way of being with each other; and great, probably convulsive social changes are needed to create these psychic changes."

You won't find Sontag in a more exalted state than that. Rarely, indeed, does she allow herself to become so agitated and unguarded, especially in the realm of the outwardly political. But that is exactly where one must interpret Sontag's politics, and exaltation, extremely carefully.

Sontag's political instincts gravitate toward the individual, in exactly the same way that she reverses the standard quasi-Marxian directions of causality in the above quote. Marxists generally want to transform consciousness as the necessary first step toward changing the world. In contrast, Sontag wants the world to change so that we can get a little more pleasure out of consciousness. Convulsive social changes, for Sontag, are but extreme measures for affecting a transformation that terminates in psychic changes. Politics means nothing if it obscures the solid core of the individual self. Her commitment to this idea gives all of her writing a Stoic ring even though she never puts forward a theory of the self or a formal ethics. It is the focus on her particular brand of pleasure that provides the key. Pleasure and the Self are so deeply intertwined in Sontag's writing that one cannot even be conceived without the other.

Writing years later, in 1982, about Roland Barthes, Sontag spoke again of pleasure and the individual self. Barthes' great freedom as a writer was, for Sontag, tied up with his ability to assert himself in individual acts of understanding. Continuing a French tradition that goes back at least to Montaigne (a man not unaware of the Stoics), she argues that Barthes' writing "construes the self as the locus of all possibilities, avid, unafraid of contradiction (nothing need be lost, everything may be gained), and the exercise of consciousness as a life's highest aim, because only through becoming fully conscious may one be free." She speaks about the life of the mind as a "life of desire, of full intelligence and pleasure."

A human mind, i.e. an individual mind, will, at its best, be "more generous" and "more humane." But for Sontag, it is what humans have access to in the world of ideas, as individual thinking agents, that marks out the highest arena of accomplishment.

"Of course, I could live in Vietnam," she writes in "Trip to Hanoi," "or an ethical society like this one—but not without the loss of a big part of myself. Though I believe incorporation into such a society will greatly improve the lives of most people in the world (and therefore support the advent of such societies), I imagine it will in many ways impoverish mine. I live in an unethical society that coarsens the sensibilities and thwarts the capacities for goodness of most people but makes available for minority consumption an astonishing array of intellectual and aesthetic pleasures. Those who don't enjoy (in both senses) my pleasures have every right, from their side, to regard my consciousness as spoiled, corrupt, decadent. I, from my side, can't deny the immense richness of these pleasures, or my addiction to them."

Sontag's political thinking is driven by the idea that what is otherwise ethical, is often thereby sequestered from what is great, and what is otherwise great, is often mired in the unethical. She never stopped worrying about this problem and she ended her life as conflicted about it as ever. It was a complication that, in the end, she embraced as one of the interesting, if troubling, things about the world.

But for a few brief moments, as the Sixties ratcheted themselves up year after year, she indulged herself in considering the possibility that the conflict between ethics and greatness could be resolved into a greater unity. She thought a little bit about revolution and totality. She got excited, exalted. Summing up thoughts about one of her favorite essays, Kleist's "On the Puppet Theater," Sontag leaves the door open for a quasi-Hegelian form of historical transcendence. She says, "We have no choice but to go to the end of thought, there (perhaps), in total self-consciousness, to recover grace and innocence." Notice the parentheses on "perhaps." She's aware that she (and Kleist) are stretching things by saying so, but she can't help allowing for the possibility of "total self-consciousness." Often, when Sontag uses parentheses she is allowing us a glimpse into her speculative, utopian side.

In "The Aesthetics of Silence" (1967), for instance, she equates the modern function of art with spirituality. She defines this spirituality (putting the entire sentence in parentheses). "(Spirituality = plans, terminologies, ideas of deportment aimed at resolving the painful structural contradictions inherent in the human situation, at the completion of human consciousness, at transcendence.)"

* * *

In the amazing, brilliant essays that make up the volume *Against*

Interpretation it is possible to discover more about the utopian side of Sontag's thinking. Drawing inspiration from Walter Benjamin, whose own ideas on art explored its radically transformative, even messianic potential, Sontag muses that, "What we are witnessing is not so much a conflict of cultures as the creation of a new (potentially unitary) kind of sensibility. This new sensibility is rooted, as it must be, in our experience, experiences which are new in the history of humanity..."

Again with the parentheses. It is as if, like Socrates, she always had a daimon on her shoulder warning her about pushing her speculations too far. But the talk of unity is an indication of the degree to which she was inspired by the events of the time, or perhaps more than the specific events of the time, by the mood and feel of the time. Her sense that there was an "opening up" of experience, sensibility, and consciousness drove Sontag to attack certain distinctions and dichotomies she saw as moribund. Again following closely in the footsteps of Walter Benjamin and his influential "Art in the Age of Mechanical Reproduction" she writes,

> Art, which arose in human society as a magical-religious operation, and passed over into a technique for depicting and commenting on secular reality, has in our own time arrogated itself a new function ... Art today is a new kind of instrument, an instrument for modifying consciousness and organizing new modes of sensibility.

This led her to a central thesis, a thesis that drove her thinking throughout the '60s, a thesis that is nestled into every essay that makes up *Against Interpretation*. She sums it up thusly:

> All kinds of conventionally accepted boundaries have thereby been challenged: not just the one between the 'scientific' and the 'literary-artistic' cultures, or the one between 'art' and

'non-art'; but also many established distinctions within the world of culture itself—that between form and content, the frivolous and the serious, and (a favorite of literary intellectuals) 'high' and 'low' culture.

Sontag's famous "Notes on 'Camp'" is simply a sustained attempt to follow that thesis through. Her defense of camp is a defense of the idea that worth can be found in areas normally, at least back in the '60s, relegated to the realm of the unserious. The new unity was going to raise everything into the realm of the intellectually interesting, and pleasurable.

Yet, Sontag is not trying to abolish all distinctions. It isn't a leveling instinct. Even in her youngest days, Sontag was suspicious of the radically democratic impulses that would, say, collapse art and entertainment. Sontag is doing something different. She is trying to show that the arena for aesthetic pleasure should be vastly expanded, but never diluted. She wants the new critical eye to stay sharp and hard. Sontag's version of pleasure is an exacting one. It is relentless and crystalline. It is an effort.

> Another way of characterizing the present cultural situation, in its most creative aspects, would be to speak of a new attitude toward pleasure ... Having one's sensorium challenged or stretched hurts ... And the new languages which the interesting art of our time speaks are frustrating to the sensibilities of most educated people.

In this, there was always an element of the pedagogue in Sontag. She was trying to teach a generation how to tackle that frustration in the name of aesthetic pleasure. She was driven by her amazing, insatiable greed for greater pleasure. She wanted us to be able to see how many interesting and challenging things there are in her world of art, a world vaster and richer than the one surveyed by the standard critical eye of her time. And, at least in the '60s, her passion for greatness and its pleasures spilled over into a yearning for a societal transformation that would make that passion and pleasure universal.

Inevitably, the exaltation and dreams of unity that she harbored during the '60s were to disappoint Sontag, as they did everyone else. She was going to have to come down from those heights and find her own version of Zagajewski's soft landing. And that is another thing that makes Susan Sontag so remarkable. At her most exalted, writing in 1968, just after returning from Hanoi, she says:

> I recognized a limited analogy to my present state in Paris in early July when, talking to acquaintances who had been on the barricades in May, I discovered they don't really accept the failure of their revolution. The reason for their lack of 'realism', I think, is that they're still possessed by the new feelings revealed to them during those weeks—those precious weeks in which vast numbers of ordinarily suspicious, cynical urban people, workers and students, behaved with an unprecedented generosity and warmth and spontaneity toward each other. In a way, then, the young veterans of the barricades are right in not altogether acknowledging their defeat, in being unable fully to believe that things have returned to pre-May normality, if not worse. Actually it is they who are being realistic. Someone who has enjoyed new feelings of that kind—a reprieve, however brief, from the inhibitions on love and trust this society enforces—is never the same again. In him, the 'revolution' has just started, and it continues. So I discover that what happened to me in North Vietnam did not end with my return to America, but is still going on.

The world did return to normalcy, if not worse. But Sontag didn't indulge in the outright lunacy of the New Left as it spiraled off into fantasyland. (Though she did endorse something of the mood of the New Left in one of her less successful and rather more hysterical essays "What's Happening in America?" (1966). Still, when the chips were down she didn't take that path. She kept her head.)

And the hint as to how she kept her cool is already there in the above passage. Her commitment to the integrity of the individual mind was a buttress for her. The solid structure of her mental edifice, built with that sternness of pleasure she never abandoned, allowed her to come in for a soft landing while people like the Situationists or the Yippies or The Weathermen floundered or came apart at the seams.

More than that, she was able to recognize her own missteps and rethink her exaltation. Even as she continued to lament the way in which her new experiences were sullied and her new consciousness never came to pass, she realized that much of its promise, especially in its political variants, had been an illusion. Increasingly in her essays in the '80s and '90s she celebrated the writers and artists of Central and Eastern Europe who fought the disaster of the "revolution." In 1997, she was to write:

> Intellectuals responsibly taking sides, and putting themselves on the line for what they believe in … are a good deal less common than intellectuals taking public positions either in conscious bad faith or in shameless ignorance of what they are pronouncing on: for every Andre Gide or George Orwell or Norberto Bobbio or Andrei Sakharov or Adam Michnik, ten of Romain Rolland or Ilya Ehrenburg or Jean Baudrillard or Peter Handke, et cetera, et cetera.

She came to see that communism in Vietnam had been a lie and a farce, even as the Vietnamese resistance to the American war machine had been noble and just. She went to Bosnia again and again and never, for even a moment, indulged in the repellant apologies for Serbian nationalism that many of her colleagues on the Left dishonored themselves with. In fact, she always saw Europe and North America's failure in Bosnia as another manifestation of the shallow interest in material happiness and comfort.

Such a vapid happiness was not what Sontag was referring to in her quest for difficult pleasure.

* * *

This is not to say that she was happy about politics and culture after the '60s. Sometimes she was outright despondent. Sometimes she felt she had been tricked. She marveled how her own arguments had come back to haunt her. Things that she had advocated for in the '60s were realized in ways completely contrary to her original intentions.

For instance in her seminal essay "Against Interpretation" (1962), she argued that criticism had become too Baroque. It was preventing immediate appreciation of things as things. So she made a call for transparence. "Transparence," she said, "means experiencing the luminousness of the thing in itself, of things being what they are." And then notoriously, at the end of the essay, she proclaimed, "In place of a hermeneutics, we need an erotics of art."

Later, she came to realize that history had pulled something of a fast one on her. People did begin to appreciate, even worship, surface and appearance. Camp moved further into the mainstream. But it wasn't happening in the way that Sontag intended. In a preface to *Against Interpretation* written in 1995 and entitled "Thirty Years Later..." she addressed the issue.

It is not simply that the Sixties have been repudiated, and the dissident spirit quashed, and made the object of intense nostalgia. The ever more triumphant values of consumer capitalism promote—indeed, impose—the cultural mixes and insolence and defense of pleasure that I was advocating for quite different reasons.

She won a battle at the expense of the greater victory she was hoping for. There was a revolution in a sense, and a democratizing of culture. But Sontag realized that it wasn't leading to pleasure, real pleasure. Instead, it led to a devaluation of the seriousness of intellect that Sontag took to be a prerequisite for genuine pleasure. In what she calls her own naiveté, Sontag, in the Sixties, made an appeal for changes that consumer culture was only too ready to provide during the next few decades. But those changes came as an empty package. Talking 30 years later about the essays of *Against Interpretation*, she says, "The judgments of taste expressed in these essays may have prevailed. The values underlying those judgments did not."

In response to this cruel trick of history, Sontag did verge dangerously close to nostalgia on occasion. Perhaps that is understandable. Her problem was even more acute than the problem of the Central Europeans for whom she had such sensitivity. Central Europeans might look back with some wistfulness on the intense seriousness of the "bad old days" but they were, still, the bad old days. For all of Sontag's hesitation in identifying with the '60s as a movement, it was during those years that she experienced her greatest pleasures in art and understanding. They weren't bad old days at all for her.

And she felt that as she was getting older she was simultaneously witnessing the disappearance of much of what had given her the greatest pleasure. In 1988, she expressed this as a European elegy. Europe, to Sontag, always represented resistance to the tide of philistinism — she even calls it barbarity — that emanates from America and its consumer culture. She says, "The diversity, seriousness, fastidiousness, density of European culture constitute an Archimedean point from which I can, mentally, move the world."

By the late '80s, she believed that that Archimedean point was drifting away as Europe became more homogeneous and "Americanized." Without naming it directly, her contempt for the idea of European integration (this, again, in 1988) is palpable. What she calls the "diversity" of Europe is predicated, for Sontag, on preserving the differences that come with national and thereby cultural boundaries. But with all the language of preservation and loss, Sontag manages to rescue the essay from outright nostalgia. She recognizes the malleability and relativity of the "idea of Europe." The idea of Europe is at its most potent, she argues, when wielded by the Central and European intellectuals who used it, implicitly, as a critique of the Soviet domination they were resisting. But Sontag is also aware that the rallying cry of "Europe" was distinctly unpalatable when raised in Western Europe as a warning against the new immigration. This latter point has only become more incisive in recent years. As always, Sontag was ahead of the times.

Indeed, by the end of her lament for Europe, Sontag turns a corner. Having aired her grievances, she begins to move forward. She comes in for another soft landing. She begins to shift onto another battlefield, moving just as quickly as modern experience does. That quickness, that readiness to move at the pace in which new experiences present themselves, allows her, in seeming paradox, to find what is solid and lasting in things. "The modern has its own logic," she writes, "liberating and immensely destructive, by which the United States, no less than Japan and the rich European countries, is being transformed. Meanwhile, the center has shifted."

Having started "The Idea of Europe (One More Elegy)" by veering into a cultural conservatism that she spoke so eloquently against in her earliest essays, she manages to steer herself back into more Sontag-like territory. She is prepared to become an exile again, as she always was in the first place. Exiled in the sense that every intellect of integrity stands alone in the last instance, as a self. In asking what will happen next, as the greatness of Europe fades and transforms, Sontag refers to Gertrude Stein's answer to those who wondered how she would deal with a loss of her roots. "Said Gertrude Stein, her answer perhaps even more Jewish than American: 'But what good are roots if you can't take them with you'."

* * *

Susan Sontag always understood the melancholic personality lingering in the back alleys of modern consciousness. She understood the will to suicide in men like Walter Benjamin. She knew why Benjamin lived under the sign of Saturn and could write:

> The resistance which modernity offers to the natural productive élan of a person is out of proportion to his strength. It is understandable if a person grows tired and takes refuge in death. Modernity must be under the sign of suicide, an act which seals a heroic will ... It is the achievement of modernity in the realm of passions.

Sontag understood the will to death and failure in Artaud. She understood the will to silence in Beckett and John Cage. Not only did she understand these things, she could write about them clearly, put her finger on them. She knew that Nietzsche's prognostication about the coming nihilism had come to pass in much of the modern, and modernist, aesthetic she cherished so dearly.

She felt the exhaustion of the modern spirit. But she wasn't exhausted by it. In her essay on Elias Canetti, "Mind as Passion," she wrote the following:

'I want to feel everything in me before I think it', Canetti wrote in 1943, and for this, he says, he needs a long life. To die prematurely means having not fully engorged himself and, therefore, having not used his mind as he could. It is almost as if Canetti had to keep his consciousness in a permanent state of avidity, to remain unreconciled to death. 'It is wonderful that nothing is lost in a mind', he also wrote in his notebook, in what must have been a not infrequent moment of euphoria, 'and would not this alone be reason enough to live very long or even forever?' Recurrent images of needing to feel everything inside himself, of unifying everything in one head, illustrate Canetti's attempts through magical thinking and moral clamorousness to 'refute' death.

Sontag is writing about Canetti but she is writing about Sontag too. As much as she measured and reported the pulse of an era in thought, art, morals... as much as she eulogized its passing, she also stood for the brute continuation of life, of pleasure, and of joy. She's dead now, but there is nothing that stimulates a desire to live more than reading one of her essays. If it so happens that we're stumbling into an age of new seriousness and new sincerity we're doing so partly because Susan Sontag showed us how important the world can be.

By Morgan Meis
26 June 2006

Sun Ra

(1914 – 1993)

In the Egyptian section of the Penn Museum stands a man. He is next to a 12-ton sphinx and is wearing a multicolored dreamcoat. His beret shimmers; a red cape hangs about his shoulders. "Planet Earth can't even be sufficient without the rain, it doesn't produce rain, you know," he tells the camera. "Sunshine... it doesn't produce the sun. The wind, it doesn't produce the wind. All planet Earth produces is the dead bodies of humanity. That's its only creation." The man pauses and slides his hand across the sphinx. "Everything else comes from outer space. From unknown regions. Humanity's life depends on the unknown. Knowledge is laughable when attributed to a human being."

* * *

The birth of Herman Poole Blount on May 22, 1914 was, for him, the least significant of all his births. Blount begat Bhlount and Bhlount begat Ra and Herman begat Sonny and Sonny begat Sun. Sun Ra left Alabama for Chicago and Chicago for Saturn, until he never quite understood how he got to planet Earth in the first place. The name 'Ra' — the Egyptian god of the sun — brought him closer to the cosmos. Each rebirth erased the one before it, until Sun Ra's past became a lost road that trailed off into nothingness. The past was passed, dead. History is his story, he said, it's not my story. My story, said Sun Ra, is mystery. Sun Ra lived life between ancient time and the future, in something like the eternal now. He told people he had no family and lived on the other side of time. Rebirth might not be the right word for the journey that Sun Ra took. Awakening is more precise, like how the ancient Egyptians were awakened. As Jan Assaman wrote in

Death and Salvation in Ancient Egypt, to be a person in ancient Egypt meant to exercise self-control. In sleep, a person is dissociated from the self. The sleeping person, then, is powerlessness, like a dead person. But the awakened one is a person risen.

> A great one is awakened, a great one wakes,
> Osiris has raised himself onto his side;
> he who hates sleep and loves not weariness,
> the god gains power...

Sun Ra believed that the whole of humanity was in need of waking up. He wanted to slough off old ideas and habits, brush off sleepy clothing and shake off drowsy food. Because present time mattered little to Sun Ra, they say he rarely slept. Even as a child, he would spend all his time playing the piano or composing. "I loved music beyond the state of liking it," he once said. Sun Ra was just as obsessed with books — you couldn't see the walls of his room for the books. Books contained words and the words held a secret code that, if unraveled, revealed truths about human existence. He read the ancient texts of Egyptians and Africans and Greeks, the works of Madame Helena P. Blavatsky (with whom he shared the initials H.P.B.), Rudolph Steiner, P.D. Ouspensky, James Joyce, C.F. Volney, Booker T. Washington. He read about the lost history of the American Negro and studied the origins of language. Sun Ra knew Biblical scripture better than any preacher, read Kabbalah concepts and Rosicrucian manifestos. Through these texts Sun Ra learned it was possible for the chaos of human knowledge to be ordered. Theosophy, relativity, mathematics, physics, history, music, magic, science fiction, Egyptology, technology — all were keys to a unified existence. Ideas and music carried a reclusive black boy from Birmingham and transported him into outer space. But the most important idea Sun Ra learned from all his reading, from all the knowledge he acquired, is how puny knowledge is in the face of the unknown. We need the unknown, Sun Ra said, in order to survive.

Sun Ra abolished sleep from his "so-called life," wrote biographer John Szwed, "just as he had come to do without the distractions of drugs, alcohol, tobacco, women." Sun Ra didn't want to be sidetracked by time like so many earthly humans, spending half their lives in a stupor of slumber. In Gurdjieff, Sun Ra read that man exists in habit, but could be awakened from his slumber with sacred songs and dances. Sun Ra vowed to live every moment in anticipation, and he would do so through jazz. Jazz was the music of the restless, the awakened. Anybody could play music on the downbeat and think, "Everything is beautiful, 'cause I'm going to heaven when I die." But peace is not an option for the fiery awakened. "Play some fire on it," Sun Ra would tell his musicians. "If you're not mad at the world, you don't have what it takes."

In jazz, unity could emerge, even as individual notes seemed in disarray and rhythms seemed uncountable. Jazz demanded discipline and precision, but also an open mind. "A lot of things that some men do... come from somewhere else," Sun Ra said, "or they're inspired by something that's not of this planet. And jazz was most definitely inspired, because it wasn't here before." Jazz was the road to a mystical experience, a sort of reasoned ecstasy. It was the music of elsewhere.

* * *

"I didn't find being black in America to be a very pleasant experience," said Sun Ra, "but I had to have something, and that something was creating something that nobody owned but us." African-Americans had always been a secret society within greater American society, with their own music, their own language, their own rituals. This secret history could be an asset for African-Americans in the Space Age to come. African-

Americans could re-invent their past and create a futurist Utopia, perhaps on a planet other than Earth, which seemed to Sun Ra unbearably steeped in chaos and confusion.

Sun Ra called his band the Arkestra, though it went far beyond the limits of a band. The Arkestra was Sun Ra's grand *Gesamtkunstwerk*, a total work that crossed the boundaries of art and life for Sun Ra and his musicians. It was Sun Ra's little Utopia. The name Arkestra itself was an allusion to the Ark of the Covenant. "A covenant of Arkestra," said Sun Ra, "it's like a selective service of God. Picking out some people. Arkestra has a 'ra' at the beginning and the end. Ra can be written as 'Ar' or 'Ra,' and on both ends of the word it is an equation: the first and the last are equal ... In the middle there is 'kest,' which equals 'kist,' as in 'Sunkist' ... I read that in Sanskrit 'kist' means 'sun's gleam.' This is why I called my orchestra 'Arkestra.'"

"Besides," Sun Ra once said, "that's the way black people say 'orchestra.'"

Arkestra performances were music, theatre, dance, philosophy. They combined the ancient and the radical future, African rhythms played with fists and synthesizers played with the elbows. Arkestra musicians followed Sun Ra's style, wearing Egyptian headdresses and African robes and Mardi Gras beads. Onstage, they laughed and danced and walked arm in arm. Sun Ra wanted to show his audiences an expression of pure possibility. And yet the Arkestra was more for the musicians than the audience. Musicians lived together (for a long while in a building Sun Ra bought on Morton Street, in the Germantown area of Philadelphia), worked together, thought together. When they weren't onstage, they were rehearsing. They played music in place of social activities, in place of sleep. The Arkestra breathed music together, abandoned themselves to it, like one single enlightened organism with Sun Ra as their guide.

Sun Ra's compositions were famously difficult, even for the most talented instrumentalists. Arkestra musicians tell stories of being baffled sometimes for months before they could hear music in the written notes. The intervals were mad, impossible. Sun Ra was patient though, often choosing musicians who were more intuitive than knowledgeable, who could be developed (intuitive people had more space in their minds). One could imagine the Morton Street building like a monastery, and Arkestra rehearsals akin to liturgical chant, with Arkestra players embodying the music through repetition until playing was an ecstatic experience. "Discipline and precision were nature's ways, the ways in which the planets spun through space, by which the birds flew; and precision rather than confusion was the answer, discipline rather than freedom," writes Szwed. Sun Ra once told an interviewer that his very reason for being on Earth (not being of Earth) was to be a teacher. People are free to think what they want, he said. They got their own minds. God just lets them go on and on and on. But people, he said, they don't ask no questions.

"If teenagers are lost," Sun Ra told another interviewer, "it is because they have been fed upon the word freedom, not discipline."

In the documentary *A Joyful Noise*, Arkestra musician James Jacson tells the story of his drum. There was a tree, Jacson says, right across the street from 5626 Morton Street. And one day this tree got hit by lightning. I had been needing a drum, Jacson says. Sun Ra suggested Jacson use some of the wood from this downed tree before the city carted it away. Jacson spent an entire summer working with the stump, hollowing it out, crafting it into a musical instrument. He carved a bas relief on the side, a verse out of the "Book of the Reawakening" (Sun Ra's name for the Egyptian *Book of the Dead*). "I didn't really know a lot about drumming," Jacson says to the camera, "but Sun Ra, of course, showed me a whole 'nother idea about drumming." Sun Ra named Jacson's drum the Ancient Infinity Lightening Wood Drum. It was a sacred object of the simplest kind, carved from an accident of nature, by a man who came to understand its possibilities just by being with it.

* * *

In her novel *The Grey World*, written ten years before the birth of Sun Ra, Anglo-Catholic mystic Evelyn Underhill wrote, "It seems so much easier in these days to live morally than to live beautifully. Lots of us manage to exist for years without ever sinning against society, but we sin against loveliness every hour of the day."

This observation reminds me of Sun Ra (who, perhaps, had read this book, having read nearly every book on mystical and occultish things printed in the English language). There was no dearth of ideas in the hundred-odd years that spanned the mid-19th to the mid-20th centuries for how to improve the lot of African-Americans, how to lift them up and give them purpose with strong leadership and values, a new moral code. Sun Ra's thoughts about the necessity for discipline and reason in African-American society were shared by a number of American intellectuals and spiritual leaders, from W.E.B. Du Bois to Elijah Muhammad. But discipline alone lacked, for Sun Ra, creative energy, vitality. When morality expressed itself in beauty, daily life had a little more of that mysterious, mystical quality to it, a quality Sun Ra was always searching for to conquer the "unpleasant" aspects of what it was to be human on Earth. Morality could make life sensible but beauty made life happy. Why wear only a black suit and tie when we have available to us all the colors of the rainbow?

"All of my compositions are meant to depict happiness combined with beauty in a free manner," Sun Ra wrote in "The Aim of My Compositions":

Happiness, as well as pleasure and beauty, has many degrees of existence; my aim is to express these degrees in sounds which can be understood by the entire world ... The mental impression I intend to convey is that of being alive, vitally alive. The real aim of this music is to coordinate the minds of peoples into an intelligent reach for a better world, and an intelligent approach to the living future.

Where Washington and Du Bois, for instance, were products of the Enlightenment, Sun Ra was a Romantic, finding order in the laws of nature and the patterns of ancient history. Sun Ra's intelligent romantic method, his intelligent reach for a better world, could have been expressed by Dostoevsky, who wrote in *Notes from Underground*:

> The characteristics of our romantics are to understand everything, to see everything and to see it often incomparably more clearly than our most realistic minds see it; to refuse to accept anyone or anything, but at the same time not to despise anything; to give way, to yield, from policy; never to lose sight of a useful practical object ... to keep their eye on that object through all the enthusiasms and volumes of lyrical poems, and at the same time to preserve "the sublime and the beautiful" inviolate within them to the hour of their death, and to preserve themselves also, incidentally, like some precious jewel wrapped in cotton wool if only for the benefit of "the sublime and the beautiful" ... The romantic is always intelligent...

What better way to preserve the sublime and the beautiful in a useful practical object than by creating a drum from a forgotten tree stump? Only in beauty could Sun Ra's ideas resolve themselves, the way mathematics can only eventually resolve into song when it is part of everyday life.

In 1979 the Arkestra put out an album called *Sleeping Beauty*. The first track on the album has the title "Springtime Again."

Sleep, for Sun Ra, was like a little death, just as it was for Sleeping Beauty. And yet Sleeping Beauty was never actually dead; she was just waiting to see the spring again. "I have to be like a little child," he said. "I have to be totally sincere — to put my music out there and say take it or leave it." Life, for Sun Ra, was not only a morality tale, but a fairytale too.

By Stefany Anne Golberg
29 April 2014

Adam Yauch

(1964 – 2012)

The Beastie Boys were a trio, a threesome. Musically, this presents certain difficulties. You could call it a theological problem. How do you unify a trinity? How do you balance the three individual voices without ending up in cacophony?

The fact that the Beastie Boys were rappers made it all the more difficult. Rappers don't sing; they rap. So harmony is out. There will be no blending of voices. No barbershop tricks were going to solve the problem for the Beasties. These three fellows from Manhattan and Brooklyn would have to develop a new style of rapping altogether. The style was perfected on their second album, Paul's Boutique, but it was already present in their debut album *License to Ill*. Maybe the fact that the Beastie Boys started almost as a gag (three white Jewish kids from New York make a rap album) had a freeing effect on their music. Taking themselves less than seriously, they were able to have a loose approach to rhythm and lyrics. They would finish one another's sentences, combining thoughts and rhymes, as if their three-partite mind was connected bodily and spiritually.

Without exactly intending to, the Beastie Boys helped solve one of rap's biggest problems in the early to mid-1980s, which was rap's simplistic rhyme scheme. Early rap can often feel like a nursery rhyme set to music. The rhyming is too often obvious and formulaic. The stress is always on the last syllable of the line. No offense to Kurtis Blow (an innovator in his own place and time), but the lyrics to his less-than-fantastic song "Basketball" are a case in point:

Basketball is my favorite sport
I like the way they dribble up and down the court

It is straight iambics all the way through, with a hard caesura and stress to end each line. In a word: boring. (Blow's thoughts on basketball did not exactly kindle the imagination either, but that is another point.) Something had to change. Circa 1986, the rap world was ready to experiment with something a little more complicated. That's the year Run-DMC came out with the album *Raising Hell*. The first cut on that album is exciting. There's no other way to describe it. It is called "Peter Piper." The funny thing is, it is a rap song about nursery rhymes. It is as if Run-DMC was saying, "OK, let's take this nursery rhyme stuff up a notch or two." In "Peter Piper," the beat is fast, the rhyming is fast, and the lines play around with long and short syllables, enjambment, off-rhymes — the works. The song starts acapella and then a stripped-down sample of Bob James' "Take Me to the Mardi Gras" kicks in. A cowbell and a little synthesizer riff on top of a simple beat. It creates a raw and insistent feel. When Run and DMC rap over the beat they don't just follow it along, as previous rappers were content to do. They jump all over the beat, as in the line, "He's the better of the best best believe he's the baddest."

> Now Dr. Seuss and Mother Goose both did their thing
> But Jam Master's gettin loose and D.M.C.'s the king
> Cause he's adult entertainer
> Child educator
> Jam Master Jay king of the crossfader
> He's the better of the best best believe he's the baddest
> Perfect timin when I'm climbin I'm a rhymin apparatus
> Lot of guts
> When he cuts
> Girls move their butts
> His name is Jay hear the play he must be nuts

There's a straight lineage from Run-DMC's "Peter Piper" to the

Beastie Boys' "Brass Monkey" on *License to Ill*. In fact, the Beastie Boys sampled directly from "Peter Piper" on another song from *License to Ill*, "The New Style." Clearly, they were paying attention. Don't get me wrong, "Brass Monkey" is a stupid song. The lyrics are verging on asinine. But they flow. Sometimes they move ahead of the beat, sometimes they fall behind it. One Beastie will start a line before the other is completely finished.

> Got this dance that's more than real
> Drink Brass Monkey — here's how you feel
> Put your left leg down — your right leg up
> Tilt your head back — let's finish the cup
> M.C.A. with the bottle, D. rocks the can
> Ad-Rock gets nice with Charlie Chan
> We're offered Moet — we don't mind Chivas
> Wherever we go with bring the Monkey with us

Simple tricks like the pause before "down" and "up" in the third line give the whole song an off-kilter jauntiness that much of previous hip hop hadn't figured out how to produce yet. And here is where the Beastie Boy uniqueness really arrived. It doesn't seem like much of a revelation on the face of it, but the Beasties started to trade vocals within a line. They realized that it sounded better if one guy said "put your left leg" and then the other guys say "down," and then the first guy comes in again with "your right leg" and the other guys finish with "up." The possibility for layering and lyrical complexity had taken a great leap forward, just like that.

You could say that Run-DMC's *Raising Hell* and the Beastie Boys' *License to Ill* are companion albums. Both groups were hitting on some of the very same ideas at the same time. In fact, Run-DMC and the Beasties knew one another by then and they were both working with producer Rick Rubin. The rap world was still small enough that an innovation by one group could be heard at a show and used by another group in a song the very next day. It was like the Dutch and Italian painters of the late Renaissance. They were competing with one another, watching one another, grabbing at the latest idea and then trying to one-up that idea in the next painting. *Raising Hell* and *License to Ill* were released within a few months of each other in 1986. By their second album, *Paul's Boutique*, the Beastie Boys had already learned from, synthesized, sampled, and moved on from what Run-DMC had thrown at them.

Once the Beastie Boys had created their own style, they applied it to music outside the hip-hop tradition. Sometimes, as on *Ill Communication*, the Beastie's would stray from rap into more of a punk/post-punk screaming style (the first version of the Beastie Boys was actually a punk band). Their 2007 album *The Mix-Up* was an all-instrumental affair. The three core members of the Beastie Boys (Mike D, Ad-Rock, and MCA) had learned to work together so well that their music eventually transcended any particular genre.

There's a track on *Paul's Boutique*, the Beastie Boys' most fully realized and brilliant album, called "Shadrach." The Beasties made a lovely animated video of the song in 1989. "Shadrach" references a biblical story from the Book of Daniel. The Beastie Boys are comparing themselves to the three pious Jews in the story: Shadrach, Meshach, and Abednego. In the Bible, these three Jews were thrown into a fiery furnace by the Babylonian king Nebuchadnezzar over their refusal to worship the Babylonian gods. They are protected from the fire by the Hebrew god, forcing Nebuchadnezzar to pardon them and to make special provisions for the protection of Jews.

"Shadrach" is by no means a religious tune. The lyrics include the lines:

It's not how you play the game it's how you win it
I cheat and steal and sin and I'm a cynic

The Beastie Boys clearly found it amusing to think of themselves as these three biblical Jews. The significance ends there. Except that there is one line from the Book of Daniel that might have resonated with the Beasties. It reads, "Then the three, as out of one mouth, praised, glorified, and blessed God in the furnace." It was very much as if the three Beastie Boys — just like Shadrach, Meshach, and Abednego — shared one mouth. And there is something miraculous about that. They were, after all, just three normal guys, school friends who decided to start a band. Where did the brilliance come from? How did these three individuals manage to come together into a unity that so transcended the individual parts? There is no way they could have known, back then, that they were meant to be together, that the three of them could give voice to a sound and a style that had never been heard before. As their collaboration developed, they would sometimes refer to themselves simply as "The Three."

The death last week of MCA (Adam Yauch) seems particularly cruel. If the universe were fair, the Three would have managed to die together. Perhaps they could have gone down in a fiery crash to match the fiery furnace of Shadrach, Meshach, and Abednego. But it didn't happen that way. Real-world stories rarely have such tidy endings. The only thing to do now is to mourn the death of one man, Adam Yauch, and thus the death of the trio of which he was one indivisible part.

By Morgan Meis
14 May 2012

Guru

(1961 – 2010)

I remember hearing Gang Starr for the first time. I was in my friend's garage, the one at his mom's house in South Central L.A. that he'd converted into a hangout spot, which was the fashion at the time. The neighborhood dogs were barking pointlessly in all the yards and the LAPD helicopters chop-chop-chopped the sky, ever present. It was a warm day, as I recall, and the sound coming out of the garage was damn smooth. I liked the raspy voice of the MC. He was rapping about the streets, which was also the fashion. He wasn't just bragging, rhyming about how hard he and his crew were. But he wasn't wagging a finger in condemnation, either. There was a balance to the song, something real from the standpoint of someone who knows. Like something Johnny Cash would have understood.

The song was "Just to Get a Rep" and the MC went by the name of Guru. Guru dropped into a coma two weeks ago after a heart attack related to his fight with cancer. On April 19, he died.

"Just to Get a Rep" might not be the best Gang Starr song, but it is the one I'll always listen to with a special fondness. One of the difficult things about doing hip hop in the late '80s/early '90s was navigating the whole gangster-rap thing. Did you try to out-gangsta the other guys? Did you go off in a completely different direction like the post-hippie sound of De La Soul? The gangsta-rap persona was a bit overwhelming for any young MC trying to create a sound and an identity. Guru understood all that. "Just to Get a Rep" had a streety edge to it; Guru was down. Still, it was clear that he saw the tragedy and ugliness of the gangster life. Plus he wore that Black Muslim cap and he'd throw out fancy words, complicated diction. Guru once rhymed "mic" with "teletype." I heard someone refer to him once as the "wise uncle." I like to think of Guru that way. Just like your wise uncle, Guru was dangerously close to being full of shit, getting a little too self-righteous. But he always reined it back in the nick of time. "Jazz Thing," the song made famous by Mo' Better Blues, is preachy and didactic but redeemed, nevertheless, by the delightful phrase, "Thelonious Monk, a melodious thunk."

Guru (and his amazing DJ, Premier) had a real ear for jazz and they pushed it into hip-hop vocabulary more successfully, arguably, than anyone else at the time. Often, Gang Starr songs would dig pretty deep into the musical tradition. What, for instance, are all those crazy space noises dancing around the baseline in the background of "Just to Get a Rep?" That's the sample from Jean-Jacques Perrey's "E.V.A." Perrey was a Frenchman who moved to New York in the '50s and started experimenting with loops and electronic noises with his new friend Robert Moog (of Moog-synthesizer fame). Perrey also cut a few albums for Vanguard with Gershon Kingsley, sometimes credited with having written the first ever electropop song ("Popcorn") and a friend to John Cage.

That's the sort of stuff Gang Starr was comfortable referencing. Musically, they were always tying hip-hop back to its roots just as Guru was doing his best to address the coherence and narrative unity of the black experience. Guru and Premier wanted young DJs to appreciate experimental electronica music and stick-up kids to think about Marcus Garvey. Probably they failed in both. Thing is, "Just to Get a Rep" still sounds great whether or not anyone ever got the message. Whenever Guru's voice pops up over a jazzy baseline, I feel like I'm hearing something that will last even though Guru himself has left the building.

By Morgan Meis
4 May 2010

Kurt Cobain

(1967 – 1994)

Nearly 20 years after the suicide of Kurt Cobain, I found myself watching this performance once again, Nirvana's rendition of Lead Belly's rendition of "Where Did You Sleep Last Night." The television played this MTV *Unplugged in New York* performance on a loop as I sat on the floor at a friend's apartment in the East Village the night Cobain was found dead at 27. "Where Did You Sleep Last Night" played over and over again. The memory is so strong that I know it must be false.

"Where Did You Sleep Last Night" was the last in the *Unplugged* set, the last song on what would be Nirvana's final album. The fragile and surprising live performance of this song is Kurt Cobain's defining moment. In a 1993 interview, not long before his death, Cobain told a reporter that he had been introduced to Lead Belly from reading William S. Burroughs. "I'd never heard about Lead Belly before so I bought a couple of records, and now he turns out to be my absolute favorite of all time in music," he said. "I absolutely love it more than any rock'n'roll I ever heard." On the MTV stage, Cobain told the audience, "This was written by my favorite performer... Our favorite performer, isn't it?" he asked his band. And then he began to strum. The tempo Cobain chose seemed almost too slow but the band did not hurry him. Unlike Lead Belly's bluesy, waltzy 1944 version, Nirvana played "Where Did You Sleep Last Night" as a dirge. There were candles all around the stage; a purple light glowed around the band. Cobain sang hunched over with his eyes nearly shut, as if were simultaneously performing and elsewhere. He sang:

My girl, my girl, don't lie to me

Tell me where did you sleep last night
In the pines, in the pines
Where the sun don't ever shine
I would shiver the whole night through

Her husband, was a hard-working man
Just about a mile from here
His head was found in a driving wheel
But his body never was found

* * *

Grunge was often defined by its negativity. It was not a rebellious negativity but a passive negation, a cancelling out. If you asked grunge what it was for, the answer was, supposedly, "Nothing." The same answer might be given if you asked grunge what it was against. This sentiment was encapsulated by Kurt Cobain's famous — and perhaps most enduring — lyric, "Oh well, whatever, nevermind." The sullen indifference (sometimes referred to as irony) of grunge — and the generation that produced it — was mind-boggling and infuriating to the generation of the 1940s, '50s and '60s, generations defined by wars and causes. Grunge had no external wars, no causes that felt immediate enough to be worth fighting for. The grunge generation was said to be internal — in other words, self-absorbed. This was true. Grunge looked mostly inward, as its war was with and about itself. Musically speaking, grunge's most direct influence was punk. But where the full-blown nihilism and shock of punk still had the touch of theater and play, grunge was all the more desperate for feeling it had nothing really to show. Punk was shredded, ripped apart, exploded. Punk was dyed in brilliant colors, adorned with metal and combat boots. Punk was furious. "Kick over the wall, cause government's to fall," sang The Clash. Grunge was torn, faded, uncombed. It was the sweater your friend found in a thrift store and annoyingly left on your floor for a month, which you decided to start wearing for lack of initiative to get your own sweater. The image of grunge was, essentially, that of a homeless person.

Punk screamed at you. Grunge called into the desolation. "Oh well, whatever, nevermind." This lyric is far from a battle cry. This is the song of despair.

The homeless despair of grunge was born of a generation that felt itself on the fringes of American life. Few people could understand how young Americans who lived in relative prosperity and peace could sing about alienation so passionately that it sounded like a crisis. What crisis was there in suburbia, in the innocuous food court of the mall? "Anti-social" and "non-aspirational" were other adjectives used but a better word, perhaps, is "bereft." What defined grunge most was a longing, a grasping for something essential but inexpressible.

Kurt Cobain liked to remember himself as a happy child in Aberdeen, who lost his joy when his parents divorced. Cobain withdrew into himself after that; he never felt quite right again. "I remember feeling ashamed, for some reason," he told journalist Jon Savage in a 1993 interview. "I was ashamed of my parents. I couldn't face some of my friends at school anymore, because I desperately wanted to have the classic, you know, typical family. Mother, father. I wanted that security, so I resented my parents for quite a few years because of that." Cobain told Savage that he became antisocial as he started to "understand the reality of his surroundings." Then, Cobain turned the conversation to genealogy. He had recently discovered his Irish ancestry, he told Savage, by calling random Americans whose name was similar to his. "I couldn't find any Cobains at all, so I started calling Coburns. I found this one lady in San Francisco who had been researching our family history for years… They came from County Cork, which is a really weird coincidence, because when we toured Ireland, we played in Cork and the entire day I walked around in a daze. I'd never felt more spiritual in my life."

When Cobain married and had a child in the last two years of his life, the question arose how it could be possible that two heroin-addicted rock musicians could raise a child. Less-considered was the very fact that two heroin-addicted rock musicians wanted so much to be a family. "I'm too sensitive," Cobain wrote to Boddah, his childhood imaginary friend on the night he shot himself in the head, "I need to be slightly numb in order to regain the enthusiasms I once had as a child ... I think I simply love people too much, so much that it makes me feel too fucking sad." Kurt Cobain's music might have been self-absorbed, but it wasn't indifferent. It was an expression of sincerity that had no place to go.

I'm worst at what I do best
And for this gift I feel blessed
Our little group has always been
And always will until the end

* * *

"Where Did You Sleep Last Night" is not Lead Belly's song. He shares it with 150 years of musicians who came before and after him. It is a folksong whose author has been lost to time, dating at least back to the 1870s, passed down from singer to singer for decades until it was printed in 1917. The song has been recorded and re-recorded, at the rate of nearly once a year since it was written, taking the form of bluegrass, blues, pop, folk, Cajun, zydeco, rock, country, and western. It is a very American song.

The lyrics of "Where Did You Sleep Last Night" change with the renditions; from the 19th century, the song has been a metaphor for exile, slavery, life in the coal mines or the Great Depression. Sometimes there is a long timeless train in the place of the decapitation, but nearly everyone sings of a cold wind, a shivering, a desolation. Who is this girl spending a long windy night sleeping in the woods, the man who loses his body? The song is all questions and no answers. "Where Did You Sleep Last Night" is mysterious, full of longing, and alienation, and a matter-of-fact despair that offers no solutions.

American music is as much the child of this despair as it is of optimism. In the 19th century, as America was really coming into her own, some musicians chose to recreate the melodies of European parades and waltzes. All the while, other music was bubbling up from the country's swamps and her deep dark pines. It was a music of homelessness, hopelessness, lost love, hard work, murder, suicide. Of course no music expresses these feelings so blatantly as the blues. With Kurt Cobain's *Unplugged in New York* performance of "Where Did You Sleep Last Night" (specifically, Lead Belly's version of the song) he was connecting grunge to its despairing American roots — you might say its rootless roots — changing himself from a rock star to a participant in the American musical tradition.

* * *

Kurt Cobain was anxious on the night of the *Unplugged* show. People said he was suffering from drug withdrawal, that he wasn't smiling, or joking, that he didn't seem to be having any fun. Earlier, Cobain had asked the show's producer to decorate the stage with stargazer lilies, black candles, and a crystal chandelier. "You mean like a funeral?" asked the producer. And Cobain replied, "Exactly. Like a funeral."

In the last verse of the song, Cobain leaned forward in his gray office chair and broke into a scream.

My girl, my girl, where will you go?
I'm going where the cold wind blows

In the pines, the pines
Where the sun don't ever shine
I would shiver the whole…

Just before he was about to finish, Cobain sighed fast and opened his eyes in one last, panicked stare, as if someone had told him a secret he never wanted to know.

After the set, Cobain wandered off the stage in a bit of a daze. He lit a cigarette, stopped by some fans in the audience to sign a few autographs. Apparently, the producers of the show wanted Kurt to go out and do an encore, but Cobain told them he was finished.

By Stefany Anne Golberg
31 March 2014

Bob Bogle

(1934 – 2009)

Chet Atkins' "Walk Don't Run" was recorded in 1957. It's a groovy little number. A soft, jazzy drum beat rumbles along beneath a wide-ranging guitar melody backed nicely by a second guitar.

In 1960, a young group called The Ventures did a remake of Chet's song. It was the same song, but it wasn't the same song at all. Musicians talk about creating a new sound or looking for that new sound. They often talk about that new sound in hushed tones, as if they've suddenly crossed over into the realm of the sacred. There's lots of nodding and smiling. Knowing glances replace anything that could be put simply into language.

In 1960, a new sound came into being. There were others getting to the same place at the same time — Dick Dale, The Shadows, Link Ray. But "Walk Don't Run" is a particular revelation because it's a re-make. You can listen to the Chet Atkins version and then The Ventures version and hear it with your own ears. The Ventures aren't covering Atkins' song, they aren't even really interpreting it. It is something more akin to alchemy. They are magically transforming one thing into another. That's how a new sound gets created. All the background elements have to be there: the music technology, the cultural mood, the various influences ready to combine. And then it just happens — the sum leaps forward to be greater than its parts. Surf music is born.

What's the difference between the two songs? It's hard to say exactly. But The Ventures' version is hollowed out and twangier. Bob Bogle is going nuts with his whammy bar. There's a spaciness to the sound, the feeling that it is coming from farther away than the Chet Atkins version. It also sounds like it could go on forever, like it's the soundtrack to something that never ends. Admittedly, though, these are not very precise thoughts.

There's a great interview in *Playboy* magazine from 1978. Ron Rosenbaum is trying to get Bob Dylan to talk about his music, a notoriously difficult task. But then Rosenbaum asks Dylan about the sound of the streets.

Dylan: That ethereal twilight light, you know. It's the sound of the street with the sunrays, the sun shining down at a particular time, on a particular type of building. A particular type of people walking on a particular type of street. It's an outdoor sound that drifts even into open windows that you can hear. The sound of bells and distant railroad trains and arguments in apartments and the clinking of silverware and knives and forks and beating with leather straps. It's all, it's all there ...

Playboy: Late-afternoon light?

Dylan: No, usually it's the crack of dawn. Music filters out to me in the crack of dawn.

Playboy: The "jingle jangle morning"?

Dylan: Right.

Dylan had the sound of the jingle-jangle morning. According to Dick Dale, the sound surf music was trying to get at was exactly that — the surf. Dale said in an interview, "I don't claim to be a musician, I didn't go to Julliard. I'm into just chopping, chopping at 60 gauge, 50 gauge strings. That's the sound, the sound of the waves chopping." Bogle himself never really liked the surf-music designation. He considered The Ventures simply to be an instrumental group with a new, twangy sound.

But the surf-music label always stuck. Maybe it was just the wide-open nature of the sound. The way that the chopping of those guitars chopped right along with the waves in the California air, a California that had yet to create its own specific sound in the rock 'n' roll of the time. Bob Bogle died last week. He was one of those rare people who hears something just over the horizon and goes running after it. He knew there was something out there. When everyone else heard The Ventures do "Walk Don't Run" they discovered something they didn't even know they'd been looking for. A new sound.

By Morgan Meis
23 June 2009

Günter Grass

(1927 – 2015)

When Günter Grass died last month, it brought back memories of 1991, of my first year in New York City. I sometimes think of this period in New York as its last dangerous days, when the city still had that anxious, patched-together sensibility, which is just another way of saying that once I lived in a New York City different than the New York City of today, a New York City that was glorious because I was young then. I lived that first year alone, in a single room on the upper floors of the 92nd Street Y. The 92nd Street Y was better known as a point-of-call for Manhattan sophisticates, who likely had little idea that, as they listened to the wisdom of celebrities in the great lecture hall, dozens of men and women were residing, like me, in tiny rented rooms on the floors above them.

I hardly saw another person during my time at the Y. When I first arrived in the fall of 1991, I would leave my room at what I thought would be sociable hours, walking through the linoleum halls to the communal kitchen or the communal bathroom, looking for company. Most other tenants did not live at the 92nd Street Y as I did; they were in New York to sightsee, staying a few weeks or so and spending most of their time on the town. Not long after I moved into the 92nd Street Y, I started eating in my room, leaving only at odd hours, to make the loneliness seem less unusual.

I had come to New York City to study theater at a famous academy, which had produced many actors of note. At eighteen, I thought the theatrical life to be a romantic profession, and that to step out onto a New York City stage as an actor was to finally be a person. It didn't matter how small the stage: the smaller the better, as a small stage was a sign of authenticity and mystique.

My school was in the middle of the island of Manhattan, on the same subway line as the 92nd Street Y. That green subway line was, in my first year, a spine from which all other parts of the city spread and I rarely strayed from that spine. Every day, five days a week, I boarded the train at 86th Street and traveled to the neo-Colonial building in Midtown where I pretended to be other people and things: a resiliently moody waitress, a mythological Greek princess, a dot. At the end of the school day, I returned to the 92nd Street Y and spent my nights alone, eating Chinese dumplings on the bare floor and listening to music on the portable cassette player I had brought with me from my hometown, along with my Third Edition *Roget's International Thesaurus* and a worn paperback copy of my favorite novel, *The Tin Drum*. When I was done eating, I would turn off the lights and sit on my bed, watching the taxis go down Lexington Avenue.

A few months into school, the holidays came. Having nowhere to go, I spent my time admiring the famous window displays on 5th Avenue and the way the city still moves fast in the cold. On Thanksgiving, I baked chocolate-chip cookies on a disposable tin sheet in the kitchen of the 92nd Street Y, put them in plastic baggies, and walked around the Upper East Side handing them out to hobos, introducing myself as I went. If a man were sleeping (they were all men), I would place the cookie bag gently next to his face, so that he would not miss it upon waking.

In late December of 1991, I broke my foot rehearsing a movement for a role. I was determined to stay on in the city and continue my artistic career, despite the huge cast on my leg, and the crutches under my arms, and the fact that it had started to snow. Every day, I pulled my body through the grey slush, made my way down the crowded steps of the subway, and took the green line to school in Midtown. There, I performed my roles as best I could, sitting in a chair or on the floor. When weekends came, I sat on my bed in the single room of the 92nd Street Y with the window wide open, to bring in the air and voices. Below me, Manhattan society mingled in the lobby as I read *The Tin Drum* under the covers.

* * *

From the moment Oskar Matzerath is born in Danzig, in 1924, he is consciously acting a part.

"I was one of those clairaudient infants whose mental development is completed at birth," says *The Tin Drum*'s protagonist, "and after that merely needs a certain amount of filling in. The moment I was born I took a very critical attitude toward the first utterances to slip from my parents beneath the light bulbs."

"He'll take over the business someday," was the utterance of his father.

"When little Oskar is three years old, we'll give him a tin drum," said his mother.

"Outwardly screaming and impersonating a reddish blue baby, I reached a decision," says Oskar. "I would reject my father's suggestion ... point blank, but when the proper time came ... I would give favorable consideration to my mother's wish."

To Oskar Matzerath, the whole world is a play in which adults predictably perform. Act One: The coarse father unintentionally belittles his mother. Act Two: The mother screams at the German father in Kashubian, which he can neither stand nor understand. Act Three: The weeping mother is consoled by her cousin/lover until, at last, everyone makes up and carries on as before. Looking for a way out of this hellish, grownup show, Oskar resolves to stop growing. The night of his third birthday, as the play is performed in the living room, Oskar puts his new tin drum safely aside. He walks to the top of the cellar stairs and hurls his body down. At this moment, Oskar not only makes himself perpetually small but dangerous and loud. At home, at school, in the street, Oskar bangs away on his tin drum to drown out the sounds of people. Oskar learns he has a scream that can shatter glass. In short, Oskar makes himself into a freak, a part that no one wants to play. His freakishness becomes his power.

In the years to come, Oskar's Danzig becomes a war zone. His neighbors sing the slogans of the Nazi party and wave little flags. His father wears an SS uniform with pride. Oskar's uncle Jan is killed in a standoff at the Polish post office; his mother commits suicide by gorging herself on fish. In his late teens, Oskar runs away to the circus where he entertains Nazi officers with his glass-shattering talents. Eventually, Oskar is accused of a crime he didn't commit and is confined to a mental institution. There, he writes the story of his life, slipping between first and third person, now referring to himself as "I" now as "Oskar."

Oskar's smallness was a barrier between himself and the rest of the world: the oafish antics of his father, the infidelities of his mother, the mocking songs of children, the traumas of war. At the same time, Oskar, conscious that he was playing at the world, was never fully in the world. He was not a child, not an adult, not a Pole, not a German, invisible and utterly conspicuous. Slipping around from one identity to another — faking life left and right like a prizefighter — may have protected Oskar from some suffering, but it also left him without any single identity to rely on. Oskar knew his freakishness was just another role, the role of "the eternally three-year-old drummer."

"Lonely and misunderstood," relates self-conscious newborn Oskar, "Oskar lay beneath the light bulbs, concluded that things would go on that way for sixty or seventy years until a final short circuit cut off all fonts of light, and so lost his enthusiasm before this life beneath the light bulbs even began ..."

* * *

At school, because I could not move well in my cast, I performed my roles stationary. Acting still, I discovered that movement is a big part of the craft. A really devoted actor can't move like someone else until first investigating how she, herself, moves. In study, an actor learns to watch herself as if she were watching a performer. Attention is drawn to her posture, her speech. She must study the way her mouth moves when she chews, how she walks, what her hands do when she is angry, what it looks like — from the outside — to walk, to chew, to feel. One's own walk is then replaced, gradually, by the character's walk, the character's inflections, the character's feelings. The actor is both subject and object.

Through deep attention, an actor can learn a lot about his or her self. This, I think, is what often makes great actors suffer. Not the inability to live in the world outside the world of make-believe, but the inability to live as one's own self once the information about one's self has been revealed. It's a subtle difference. Many people simply perform life, without ever knowing how they do it, without asking why, maybe without needing to know why. Acting, on the contrary, turns life into layers of witnessing. Onstage, the actor watches the actor who performs the character who is, in turn, watched by an audience. Offstage, actors must let go of the watching and just be. Actors must learn to reintegrate their self-awareness back into themselves, in order to become whole again.

Maybe there is, at the core of every actor, an unbridgeable rift between the watcher and the watched, a permanent seat on the sidelines of one's own life. Maybe this is why New York City, the great theater capital, is called the City of Dreams.

* * *

How exactly did I break my leg rehearsing for a part? I've asked myself this question many times over the years. The more I've considered it, the more puzzling the whole episode seems. I think, reflecting after all these years, that some part of me was looking for a way out. Not completely out, not so out that I would have to leave the city, or join the kids in Tompkins Square Park, or the hobos off Lexington, but just enough to keep me on the sidelines, much as I had been in my hometown. My broken leg protected me; it kept me from being a full participant in both my acting classes and New York City. It ensured that I would stay small. My injury was a bulwark against the real New York City, and a protection for the New York City of my dreamworld.

* * *

In 2006, Günter Grass published a memoir called *Peeling the Onion*. In it, the writer revealed to the world a secret: that he had been conscripted into the Waffen-SS when he was only 16 years old. Until then, it was assumed that Grass had been too young to be actively involved in the Nazi party. For Grass' entire illustrious career, he had remained silent about this episode. He had hidden behind his youth. Unlike Oskar, who decided he would act small so that he could feel big, Grass decided to act big in order to remain small. Grass' protection — and his wound — was silence. All his life, Grass used silence so that he could play his role: the role of an important, uncompromised writer.

In 2013, on the occasion of *The Tin Drum*'s 50th anniversary, the BBC interviewed Grass. At one point in the interview, a listener asked Grass why he made Oskar a dwarf. "Germany," emphasized the listener, "is by no means a land of short people."

Grass answered. It took a long time to find the right perspective from which to tell the story, he said. "I needed a person who was not involved, like a boy, but inside like a grownup, understanding everything." From a dwarf's perspective, the story of Nazi Germany could be told by someone who was implicated and, at the same time, innocent.

Oskar, for Grass, was not made small to be a witness. He wasn't a simple a "victim," a "loser" (as the Nobel Committee expressed). Oskar, Grass told the BBC, was a mirror, "a mirror to all the things that happened."

"The behavior of people in Germany, you understand," said Günter Grass, "was of a people who were not really grown up."

"I was not lucky enough," Grass told the BBC, "to stop my growing when I was three years old."

Even though it was right below me, I only attended one event at the 92nd Street Y during that first year in New York. It was a screening of Volker Schlöndorff's film version of *The Tin Drum*. I liked it, but I remember being surprised that the film left out Oskar's consignment to the asylum. You never see how Oskar, after deciding at the graveside of his father that he can and must grow, remains a freak nonetheless. This, to me, is an essential part of Grass' story, that no matter what role Oskar wanted to play, it would have to be a small one.

By Stefany Anne Golberg
8 June 2015

Contemporary culture has eliminated both the concept of the public and the figure of the intellectual. Former public spaces – both physical and cultural – are now either derelict or colonized by advertising. A cretinous anti-intellectualism presides, cheerled by expensively educated hacks in the pay of multinational corporations who reassure their bored readers that there is no need to rouse themselves from their interpassive stupor. The informal censorship internalized and propagated by the cultural workers of late capitalism generates a banal conformity that the propaganda chiefs of Stalinism could only ever have dreamt of imposing. Zer0 Books knows that another kind of discourse – intellectual without being academic, popular without being populist – is not only possible: it is already flourishing, in the regions beyond the striplit malls of so-called mass media and the neurotically bureaucratic halls of the academy. Zer0 is committed to the idea of publishing as a making public of the intellectual. It is convinced that in the unthinking, blandly consensual culture in which we live, critical and engaged theoretical reflection is more important than ever before.